THE **BIG FIVE** *for* **LIFE**

OTHER WORKS BY JOHN P. STRELECKY

The Why Café

Life Safari

Big Five for Life™ (cd series)

How to be Rich and Happy (Co-author)

THE
BIG FIVE
for LIFE

JOHN P. STRELECKY

ASPEN LIGHT PUBLISHING

THE BIG FIVE FOR LIFE. Copyright © 2007, 2012 by John P. Strelecky

Printed in the United States of America.

Publication Data

Strelecky, John P.
    The Big Five for Life / John P. Strelecky. — Aspen Light Publishing ed.
    ISBN-13: 978-0-9834896-1-0 (hardcover)

Aspen Light Publishing Edition 2012
St. Martin's Press Edition 2008

Published by Aspen Light Publishing

Inquiries to the publisher can be directed to:
Aspen Light Publishing
13506 Summerport Village Parkway Suite #155
Windermere, FL 34786

The author can be reached through
www.bigfiveforlife.com

10   9   8   7   6   5   4   3   2   1

To all the Thomas Derales of the world.

Acknowledgments

A HEARTFELT THANK-YOU TO THE MORE THAN ONE hundred dedicated people whose insights and perspectives helped mold this story into what it is.

I particularly want to thank the following individuals for their dedication and time: Matt Blauvelt, Brad Borchers, Ken Mayer, Rachel Hutter, Gabe Esparza, Tricia Crisafulli, Uwe Alschner, Peter Dunkhorst, Sijbe Bonsma, Baukje Bonsma, Alan Jaquith, Arnie Follendorf, Avril Reed, Kelly Sabourin, Barbara Harrington-Marut, Bridgett Arnold, Chris Ockwell, Karen A. Serunian, Dave Powelson, Douglas Machiridza, Pernille Fletcher, Frank LaTorre, Gid Herman, Glenn Turner, Michelle Boulton, Johnny Valentin, Jane Hall, Jim Compton, Joachim Röttinger, Kelly Moore, Kevin Sabourin, Kevin Naya, Kevin W. McCarthy, Randolph Ching, Kristen Hallett Rzasa, Marc Manieri, Kathryn MacVicker, Michael Rosen, Michele McAfee Glowth, Jeanette Cake, Norman Bryan, Ingo B. Gross, David Spencer, Bob Steiner, Suzanne Le Breton, Terry L. Brock, Vanessa Mejia, Andrea Susanne Luise Reutner, Denise McLean, Elizabeth Diaz, Jaime Shearer, Jan Mossfeldt, Paul Dillon, Joe Hinkle, Krissy Morency, Kevin O. Sullivan, Kristi Karst Gomen, Linda Brown,

Matt Ficarelli, Dr. Matthew Norton, Michael C. Zari, Michelle Lamont, Bob Warren, Tanja Sölkner, Kevin Boulton, Michael Tellone, David Wunderlin, Dave Fletcher, Sue Wilson, Bob Clark, Dawn Werner, Barb McNaughton, Barbara Pickren, Mark Dunbar.

A special thanks also to Doris Michaels and Delia Berrigan Fakis of the DSM Literary Agency for all their assistance, and to my wife, Xin, for trusting in me when I knew this was a story worth telling.

Preface

In hundreds of history books and countless museums around the world, you can learn about leaders. Most of what you will learn is how to be a bad one. Who killed the most people? Who rose to the top through treachery and deceit? Who built the biggest temple on the backs of slave labor? Apparently it makes for interesting human character studies. The problem is, it provides us with a lousy source of mentors.

In our current world, the Internet, magazines, newspapers, and television news reports carry the latest examples of bad leadership. Which persons falsified earnings reports and left thousands of their own employees with zeroed-out retirement accounts? Who took millions in payoffs and then fled their country leaving the very people they were supposed to represent in poverty? Who received multimillion-dollar bonuses despite laying off thousands of people because they failed to meet their own stated financial goals?

So where do we turn to learn about what it means to be a great leader?

We turn to the ones whose story often isn't told, the ones who are busy doing amazing things all over the world. I know they exist, because on a cold and snowy morning on a train platform in Chicago, I met one of them. His businesses made fortunes, his employees loved him, and when necessary, his customers would wait weeks just to interact with his companies.

His name was Thomas Derale. He died tragically at just fifty-five years of age, and even in that—the act of dying—he inspired everyone around him. This is a story about who he was, how he led, and the way he left this world. These are the secrets he taught me.

—Joe

Chapter One

I EASED THE PACK OFF MY SHOULDERS AND SET IT down on the ground. *Spectacular*, I thought, as I looked out at the view before me. *Truly spectacular.* The women I'd met on the train were right. The climb was difficult, but definitely worth the effort. I reached down and eased the water bottle from its place in the side mesh compartment of my pack and took a long drink.

Below me stretched miles of mountain peaks and valleys. I could make out small farming villages in some of the more open areas. Dense forests like the one I'd climbed through filled the sides of most of the mountains. I hadn't planned on taking time out to do this hike, but the Australian backpackers I'd met on the train had raved about it. I was glad I'd listened to their advice.

Suddenly, Thomas flashed through my mind yet again. *There must be something big going on with him and Maggie,* I thought. *He's crossed my mind a dozen times this morning. I need to get on e-mail tonight and see if there's a message from him.*

Over the last few years, I'd learned when someone crossed my mind with the surprising frequency Thomas was crossing mine today, something was going on with him or her. It was almost always good news.

I looked out at the view again and drew in a long breath of the pure air. I was in the midst of a four-month trip across Spain, and it had been filled with moments like this. Great architecture, friendly people, breathtaking scenery . . . *This is what it's all about,* I thought. *Like Thomas says, every day a little higher up the ascending life curve. Every day, further progress toward my Big Five for Life.*

Chapter Two

MAGGIE DERALE TOOK THE CALL FROM THE DOCTOR'S office. Her husband was sleeping soundly, which had become a rarity of late, and she didn't want to wake him. As she listened to the person on the other end of the phone, she had to bite her lip to keep from crying. "Yes," she said. "I understand. . . . Yes, I'll make sure he is there tomorrow. . . . No, I don't think there's anything you can do."

She hung up and sat down in one of the kitchen chairs. She and Thomas had picked out the kitchen set almost twenty years earlier on one of their annual vacations. At the time he'd teased her about the outrageous seat covers she selected for them. It had become a constant source of laughter ever since. That memory raced through her mind and she began to cry. It was soft tears at first, but then they came in a torrent and she sobbed with the realization of just what was happening.

When the tears stopped coming, Maggie decided there would be no more tears, not now. She picked up the phone. "Hello, Kerry, it's Maggie. . . . No, I'm afraid not. It's what they thought. . . . I know, Kerry, I know. . . . Me too. . . . Kerry, I want you to go forward with your idea. Put all your time and energy into it. I'll get my part done and get it to you in the next week. And, Kerry . . . you won't have a lot of time."

After she hung up, she went into the den and logged on to her e-mail. *I need to reach Joe*, she thought.

Chapter Three

I WALKED INTO THE SMALL INTERNET CAFÉ AND sat down at one of the terminals. I had spent the afternoon descending from the mountains and working my way back to the town where I was staying. Thomas had been on my mind almost constantly. So often in fact, I decided to check my e-mail before even heading back to my hotel or grabbing dinner. *He must have some great news*, I thought.

"Hey, Joe."

I turned and looked to my left. "Hey," I replied, and smiled. It was one of the women who had recommended the hike I'd just taken.

"Thanks for the great tip about that hike. It was spectacular."

I turned back to the monitor in front of me. The cursor twirled on the screen as I waited for the Internet browser to launch. The café was crowded with other backpackers and even a few local residents. *It never ceases to amaze me*, I thought. *Not that long ago the Internet didn't even exist, and now you can instantly communicate with people all over the world.* I logged into my account and clicked on the in-box. Sure enough, there was a message from Thomas. Actually it was from Thomas's wife, Maggie, which wasn't all that unusual. She often sent out news that pertained to both of them. I clicked the message and waited while it loaded. In a moment I saw five words that made my heart sink.

"Thomas is sick, please call."

I loaded up my online account and pulled the headphone from the hook on the side of the computer. As I typed in the numbers for the Internet phone call, my mind was racing. *What could be going on? Thomas was never sick.* I heard ringing on the other end of the line, and then Maggie's voice.

"Hi, Maggie, it's Joe. I got your message, what's going on? How's Thomas?"

"Not good, Joe." I could hear Maggie's voice tremble a bit. "I'm sorry to contact you on your travels, but I thought you would want to know."

"Know what?" I felt my chest tighten as I waited for her answer.

"Thomas is dying, Joe."

"He's what?" I asked, surprised. I couldn't believe what I'd just heard.

"He's dying, Joe. The symptoms started about three months ago. I just got the call from the doctor and they confirmed it. He has a brain tumor. It's too large for them to operate."

I tried to process what Maggie was saying. "What about something else, some other form of treatment? How about radiation or chemotherapy? There must be something."

Maggie was quiet on the phone. "No, we've asked about all those. There's nothing else they can do, Joe. It's too far along. Thomas is dying."

I spoke with Maggie for a few more minutes, then hung up. I couldn't believe it. Not Thomas. He was the epitome of health. I clicked online to find the number for my airline and then placed another call. I needed to get back to the United States.

Chapter Four

I PUT MY PACK INTO THE OVERHEAD COMPARTMENT and sat down in my seat on board the 777. The news about Thomas still hadn't completely sunk in. I knew it was true, and yet for some reason it didn't seem real. When I'd seen him a few months earlier, he was fine. How could he suddenly be dying?

I nodded to the woman sitting in the seat next to me and closed my eyes. My fingers worked slow circles around my temples.

"Are you okay?" It was the woman I'd just nodded to.

I opened my eyes and looked at her. "Yes, thanks. I just received some bad news. A friend of mine is very sick. The doctors say he's dying."

"Oh." My answer had caught her by surprise. "I'm sorry. I didn't mean to intrude."

"No, it's okay. . . . I mean it's not okay. . . . His situation isn't okay," I tried to explain. "But I can't do anything about it right now. I'm not sure I can do anything about it at all, but I want to get back to talk with him. To help out if I can."

I looked at her. She appeared to be in her late thirties. She had a pretty face, shoulder-length brown hair, brown eyes, and sharp angular features. I extended my hand. "I'm Joe. Thanks for asking if I was okay."

"Sonia," she replied, and shook my hand. "Nice to meet you, Joe. And you're welcome. Listen, I really didn't mean to intrude. If you want to just shut down for the next twelve hours and be alone with your thoughts, I totally understand."

I shook my head. "No. Thanks for that, but no."

We both sat in silence for a few moments. "Who's your friend?" she asked. "The one who's sick?"

"His name is Thomas. Thomas Derale. He's the greatest leader in the world." It was an odd way to describe someone, especially someone who was your friend, but that's what I thought of when I thought of him.

"That's an unusual description."

"I know. He's a lot of other things as well. But above everything else, that's how I always think of him."

"How did the two of you become friends?"

"That's a long story."

She smiled. "We've got twelve hours ahead of us, Joe, and I'm an avid listener."

I returned the smile. "Alright." I nodded. "It began when Thomas asked me a little question about a museum."

Chapter Five

I'D ARRIVED AT THE OUTDOOR TRAIN STATION AT 6:47 a.m. This was the first leg of a three-part commute I made every Monday through Friday. The trip began from my condominium on the upper north side of Chicago and included a walk to the train station, a ride on the train, and then another walk from the stop where I got off at, to my office.

Chicago is a great walking city in the spring and summer. If they could just move the equator north by about eight hundred miles, everything would be perfect. Unfortunately, it wasn't spring or summer. It was February, and the temperature was hovering around ten degrees, with a windchill of about negative two.

My day had begun at 5:40 a.m. with my alarm going off announcing a new day of fun. Well, not really fun—work. I shivered my way to the shower and stood under the hot water hoping that by some freak of nature when I got out it would be a Saturday, not a Monday. That had happened to me one time as a kid. I'd gotten up, taken a shower, gotten dressed, and gone downstairs only to realize it was the weekend and I didn't have to go to school.

In this case, no such luck. After a bowl of cereal and cup of coffee, I dressed in a dark blue suit, light blue shirt, sharp-looking power tie, and headed out the door. A chilly ten-minute walk down Armitage Avenue later, I was standing on the train platform.

That's when Thomas looked at me, nodded, and asked, "Is it a good museum day morning?"

As it would turn out, it *was* a good museum day morning, although at the time I had no idea what that meant. It was a good museum day morning because that was the day I met Thomas.

I didn't actually even answer him coherently when he asked me the question. Or at least I don't think I did. Most strangers don't converse when they're standing on the train platforms, especially when the windchill is minus two degrees. So Thomas kind of surprised me with both his actions and his question. I think I sort of grunted a response or uttered something very intelligent like "Uh-huh" and then gave that smile you give when you sort of hear someone say something to you, but you don't really know what he means.

When the train pulled up, we each got on. We were in opposite sides of the car though, and so our conversation ended where I had left it on the platform—with my profound "Uh-huh."

Something about Thomas, though, made me think about his question that entire day. He had been wearing a long, black wool overcoat, gloves, and no hat. His hair was cut relatively short, professional-like, and he had presence. You know how some people just command a room when they walk into it? Thomas had that, even at 6:47 a.m. on a train platform full of strangers in the middle of a Chicago winter.

Chapter Six

SONIA LOOKED UP AT ME. "SO WHAT HAPPENED with Thomas?"

"Well, I watched for him every morning the rest of that week. His question was nagging me. What the heck was a 'museum day morning'? But he wasn't there.

"After a weekend of two very loud parties, many Grey Goose martinis, and an incredibly tenacious Sunday hangover, I had pretty much forgotten about Thomas's question. That is, until I walked up the steps to the train platform on Monday morning and saw him standing there. He stood out like a beacon. His attire wasn't that different, his briefcase could have been anyone's. It wasn't that. The guy just had presence."

I WALKED up to him and extended my hand. " 'Morning, I'm Joe."

He shook it. "Good morning, Joe, my name's Thomas."

"Thomas, this is probably going to sound a little crazy, but last week, last Monday actually, did you ask me something about a museum?"

He smiled. "I did, Joe. I asked you if it was a good museum day morning."

I nodded. "Well, I have to admit, although I have no idea what that means, your question has been going through my head for the last seven days. Well, at least five of the seven. Martinis have been going through for the last two. What did you mean by a 'museum day morning'?"

Thomas smiled again. "That's kind of an unusual story, Joe. Are you sure you're that interested?"

"I am," I replied, as our train pulled up to the platform and the doors slid open.

I LOOKED at Sonia. "For some reason, I actually was that interested. It was the strangest thing. I would meet people every day in my job and in my social life, and for the most part, none of the conversations were really that interesting. I often pretended I was interested, but this time, I actually was.

"One of the reasons I'd ride an early train to work was because they were less crowded than the ones a bit later in the morning. There's something about getting smashed into a small container of complete strangers for thirty minutes of public transportation chaos that starts the day off all wrong.

"That particular morning the train was even less crowded than usual, and Thomas and I took two seats next to each other. He began our conversation with a question."

* * *

"Joe, do you know how long most people's lives last?"

I shrugged my shoulders. "Oh, I don't know, seventy years, maybe eighty."

"You're close. The average human in the United States lives around 28,500 days, or about seventy-eight years. Hopefully it ends up being more, sometimes it ends up being less, but statistically speaking, it's about 28,500 days."

His answer sort of surprised me. "I've never really thought of it in days before," I replied. "It seems shorter for some reason when you think of it in days versus years."

"Yes, it does. It makes it more real."

"Okay, so the average life is 28,500 days. What does that have to do with a museum day morning?"

"Have you ever been in a history museum, Joe? Ever wandered the halls looking at old photos of people? Shots of them at work, or in their military uniform, maybe some family photos or some goofing-off shots with friends?"

I nodded. "Sure."

"Well, one day I was in Orlando, Florida, for a conference. I ended up driving around and found this little museum in a place called Winter Garden, Florida. The whole museum can't be more than a thousand square feet, but it's filled with pictures of people from the town's history, stories of what they've done, and events that have occurred over the last one hundred and fifty years or so. And while I was wandering through that museum, it struck me. What if every day of our life was cataloged? The way we felt, the people we saw, how we spent our time. And at the end of our life a museum was built. It was built to show exactly how we lived our life."

I looked at Thomas, confused.

"Think of it this way, Joe. If eighty percent of our time was at a job we didn't like, then eighty percent of the museum would be dedicated to showing us unhappily spending our time at a job we didn't like. There would be pictures and quotes and little video monitors where people could pick scenes of different unhappy moments. If we were friendly with ninety percent of the people we interacted with, it would show that. But if we were angry and upset or yelled at ninety percent of the people we interacted with, it would show that. Those also would be documented with photos and little video clips and audios.

"If we loved the outdoors, or spending time with our kids or friends, or celebrating life with our significant other, but only spent two percent of our life fueling those loves, then no matter how hard we wished it to be different, only two percent of our museum would be dedicated to that. Maybe there would be just a few pictures in a frame at the end of a long hallway.

"Imagine what it would be like to walk through that museum toward the end of our life. To view the videos, listen to the audio, look at the pictures. How would we feel? How would we feel knowing for the rest of eternity, that museum would be how we were remembered? Every person who walked through it would know us exactly as we truly were. Our legacy would be based not on how we dreamed of living, but how we actually lived.

"Imagine if heaven, or the afterlife, or however you think of what life is like after we die, actually consists of us being the tour guide for our own museum—*for all of eternity.*"

He paused for a moment. "That's why I asked you if it was a good museum day morning."

Chapter Seven

I LOOKED AT SONIA. "I DON'T REALLY KNOW what I expected when I asked Thomas about his original question, but trust me, I never expected anything like what he shared with me."

Sonia looked awed. "That's an amazing concept, isn't it? Wow. Talk about looking at your life from a different perspective. How did you respond?"

"Oh, I think I said something smart and snappy like 'Uh-huh.' "

Sonia laughed again. "No, you didn't."

"Yeah, I'm pretty sure I did. Keep in mind this guy was a total stranger. At the time I was thinking, 'Who asks that kind of a question to some random stranger and then has this type of discussion?' "

"So what did you do?"

"I pretty much asked him that."

"And?"

"He looked me in the eye and said, 'I do.' Knowing Thomas as I do now, that doesn't seem strange at all. He's not afraid to take a conversation where most people won't. His take is that those 28,500 days are too short for small talk. At the time, though, it definitely threw me."

"What happened next?"

"I pulled it together enough to ask him why he asked people the museum question. His response was he liked to meet interesting people, and he'd found the museum question was often a good way to do it. So then I asked him if he asked the question of everyone he met, and he said no, sometimes he did, but most of the times he didn't. He said he trusted his instincts. It was his next comment, though, that really kicked off our friendship."

"What was it?"

"I asked him if that meant I was interesting, since he had asked me the question. He smiled at me and said, 'I'm starting to doubt my instincts.' He said it so totally straight-faced that at first I thought he was serious. Then he started to laugh, and I started to laugh, and a great friendship began."

Sonia smiled. "Did he ever really explain why he picked you?"

I nodded. "Years later I asked him about it. He said he saw in me what he'd seen in some others and used to see in himself every morning when he was younger. Tremendous hope, tremendous opportunity, and both of them covered with quiet desperation."

Sonia shook her head in admiration. "Wow. This guy sounds like something else."

"He is. I wasn't kidding. When I think of him, I think of the greatest leader in the world."

"I thought you said he was your friend. That description makes him sound like your boss. Do you work for him?"

"No. That's one of the things that makes Thomas the great leader he is. Everyone in his companies knows the journey the company is on, and everyone is in it together. You don't work *for* Thomas, you work *with* him."

"Seriously?"

"Seriously. He's created a culture where you're either in or you're out. If you're in, then you're part of the journey. People have different roles and get paid different salaries, but there's not the standard boss-and-subordinate separation. Like I said, you're either in or you're out."

"And that works?"

"It works for his companies. He's made fortunes from them, as have the people who work with him."

Sonia raised her eyebrows slightly in a look of surprise. "Hmm. Okay, well, back to my earlier question. Since you don't work *for* him, do you work *with* him?"

"I do. A few times each year. I have a lot of flexibility in my schedule. And, actually, just so you know, working with Thomas isn't really work."

"Excuse me? You don't work?" She smiled. "No wonder people think he's such a great leader."

"Nope, it's not like that."

"But you just said . . ."

"I know. It sounds complex but it's actually pretty simple. That's another thing that makes Thomas such a great leader. He makes leadership simple."

Chapter Eight

I SMILED. "I'VE GOT AN IDEA. DO YOU WANT TO meet Thomas?"

Sonia tilted her head and raised one eyebrow. "When?"

"Right now." I reached into the seat pocket in front of me and took out my iPhone. "This is something Thomas created a long time ago and we just updated to be downloadable." I touched the screen a few times until I found the file I was looking for, then handed Sonia the iPhone headphones.

"What am I listening to?" she asked, and put the headphones in her ears.

"Watching, actually. It's Thomas. When he created his first company, he wrote down his philosophy on leadership and on creating a successful organization. Over the years it was turned into audio, and now video."

"Cool."

I smiled. "Wait till you watch it."

I pushed play and in a moment Thomas's image came on the screen. He smiled, and although Sonia was wearing the headphones, when he started to speak, I could hear the faint sound of his voice.

"Hello, everyone, my name is Thomas Derale. I'm touched you are taking time out of your life to watch this. I hope what I'm about to share with you inspires you in some way. It has been a powerful piece of my life ever since it came to me many years ago.

"Before I began my first company, I spent quite a lot of time thinking about what I wanted the company to be like and who I wanted to be as a leader. I also gave a lot of thought to how I could narrow down my philosophy of leadership into something easy for others to understand and easy for me to explain. Finally, one evening I was sitting in my home office and looking at the pictures on my walls, and it hit me.

"Ever since I was a kid, I've been a traveler. When I was young, I loved to get on my bike and ride to places I'd never been. I'd wander the woods near my house and explore trails and creek beds and collect tadpoles. . . . I never gave too much thought to why I did those things. I just liked them, so whenever possible, I did them.

"As I grew up, I dreamed of seeing the world. Although I buried that dream for a while, eventually I uncovered it and have now traveled to many places around the globe.

"That day, when I looked at the pictures on my walls—pictures of my wife and me in different locations around the world—and I thought about my childhood adventures, I realized I've always viewed life as a journey. Whether we like it or not, from the day we are born, until the day we die, our lives are always going *somewhere*, and we are always doing *something*.

"I have a friend who owns a tiny little café out in what he refers to as 'the middle of the middle of nowhere.' And he shared with me one time the importance of finding one's own personal Purpose For Existing, or PFE as he likes to refer to it. It's our own answer for the reason why we're here, why we were born . . . why we exist. That was a powerful experience for me and one I never forgot. I liked the image of each individual person having a reason why they are alive, a purpose for their existence.

"And as I thought about my beliefs on leadership, and on life being a journey where we have the opportunity to fulfill our own personal Purpose For Existing, it all came clear to me. In addition to every person having their own PFE, every company does too. It may or may not be clearly defined, but nonetheless, there is a reason why every company exists.

"So instead of having a personal Purpose For Existing I tried to fulfill on Saturdays, Sundays, and when I felt energetic enough after a day at work. And then have a completely different corporate PFE I worked toward for long hours during the week. Why not create and lead a company where the company's Purpose For Existing was aligned with my own Purpose For Existing?

"If my PFE was the point on the horizon I wanted my life to be heading for—the destination for my journey—then it made sense to start a company whose Purpose For Existing was that same point on the horizon. Or at least a point in the same direction.

"I reasoned if I could accomplish that, then I'd enjoy my time at work more. I wouldn't be regularly dealing with an internal battle between my work direction and my life direction. They'd be aligned. My time at work would be as helpful to me in fulfilling my PFE as was my time away from work.

"Through my previous experiences, I had proven I could be very successful in business when my work and my life were not aligned. Logically then, I figured I would be exponentially more successful if they were.

"I made a related decision regarding who I'd bring into my company. I wanted people who were not only intelligent and capable, but who were also driven. And I wanted them driven by the most powerful forces possible. So starting way back then, and it has continued through today as a standard practice in all of my companies, I only hire people if their personal Purpose For Existing is aligned with the PFE of the company they want to work for.

"That single decision, more than any other in my history as a leader, is the one that has enabled me to achieve tremendous success. In my companies, I don't have people who work for me. We are all working together toward a common purpose. We are fellow travelers helping each other journey towards a similar point on the horizon. When I succeed, they benefit. When they succeed, I benefit.

"There are two ways to launch and lead a company. The first way is to start with a successful business model and layer on top of it enough perks so people are willing to work there. You can achieve success doing that. It's the way most organizations are started and run.

"But to achieve remarkable success, you do it the opposite way. You start with the ultimate job perk—the opportunity to get paid for doing what fulfills you, what provides you with a true sense of purpose as it relates to your own personal Purpose For Existing. Then you layer on top of that the most successful business models that exist."

Chapter Nine

I PUSHED A BUTTON ON THE IPHONE AND THE image stopped and the audio turned off.

Sonia took a long sip from the bottle of water sitting on her tray. I looked over at her. "Sorry, Sonia, did I bore you with that?"

"Not at all." She smiled. "That was amazing, actually. I paused because you've really got me thinking. I was in Barcelona for an executive-leadership summit my company sent me to. Barcelona was incredible, and yet I think what I've learned in the last thirty minutes is more useful than what I learned in three days at the summit."

She removed the headphones and handed my iPod back to me. "Where does Thomas come up with these ideas?"

"One of the things I learned early on from Thomas—one of the simple things he does that makes him a great leader—is he is constantly learning. When he sees something he likes at another company, he implements it in his own. A lot of the great things he's done are his ideas. A lot of them are borrowed. For example, it was Thomas's idea that he and the people he brought into his companies would only spend time on things that fulfilled their Purpose For Existing and Big Five for Life—"

Sonia interrupted me. "What's the Big Five for Life?"

"Right, sorry. It's an enhancement Thomas added to his Purpose For Existing technique and philosophy. Hold that thought regarding the Big Five for Life for a few minutes and I'll give you the whole story if you want it."

"Okay."

"So as I was saying, it was Thomas's idea that he and the people he hired would only spend their time getting paid to do things that fulfilled them. The question was, what could he do to establish that as part of the culture at his company?"

"And?"

"And he found part of his solution in the entertainment industry. He was visiting a friend of his who works at Disney World, and she mentioned that instead of being called employees, everyone who works for the Disney Company is called a 'cast member.' The idea is since Disney is in the entertainment business, then everyone who is on the company payroll is part of the Disney 'show.' Everyone at every minute has the chance to impact a guest's experience. For example, here's something Thomas saw happen all the time when he was there.

"Someone would be walking by and see a guest taking a picture. Now, if you were an 'employee,' and you were getting paid to do clerical accounting work, or empty trash cans, or run the finance division, you would probably walk right past. But since these people are 'cast members' and part of the show, no matter what they get paid to spend the majority of their time doing, when they see a guest taking a picture, the expectation is they ask the person if they would like to be in the picture, and then *they* take it."

Sonia nodded. "Interesting."

"It is, and effective too. So Thomas adopted it. He used his philosophy of a journey to help create a picture in his people's minds of what being a member of his company was all about. And then he never called people employees. He decided since the people in his companies were on a common journey together, it made more sense for people to think of themselves and each other not as employees, but as fellow travelers."

Sonia nodded again. "Did it work? I can picture some of the skeptics in my company looking at that and thinking it's foolish, or pointless."

"First of all, it definitely worked. It still is working. Words are powerful things that either support us or obstruct us. One of Thomas's favorite quotes is from a character in a book who says, 'If we say the same words often enough, even our mind starts to believe they are true.' His take is, why not say something positive—versus average, or even worse, negative.

"I don't know of anyone who draws a positive reaction from the word *employee*. At best it creates an average emotional response. But a traveler on a journey? That's something people view in a positive way. That's something they want to be a part of.

"Also, Thomas has found it to be a great screening mechanism. In general, people who think the concept of being a traveler instead of an employee is foolish, also don't mind spending their time on work that doesn't fulfill them. Thomas doesn't want those types of people in his companies. It's bad for morale, and it's bad for productivity."

Sonia looked at me, surprised. "Productivity? That sounds like a very profit-focused word for a guy who seems so focused on the softer side of business."

"Did you just say the softer side of business?"

Sonia paused. "Yes . . ."

I nodded and smiled. "Okay . . ."

"What?" Sonia smiled back at me. "That's what they call it. You know, the soft skills, the people things."

"Who is 'they'?"

"I don't know . . ." She laughed. "You know what I'm talking about."

I leaned toward Sonia. "Do you want to know a secret?"

She laughed again. "Sure."

"All the hard profits are tied up in the people things. They're not separate, and they're definitely not soft. And I'll prove it to you."

Chapter Ten

"OKAY, PROVE IT," SONIA SAID.

"Do you want the statistics or the examples?"

"Both would be great."

I laughed. "Both it is. Before I do that, though, let me tell you Thomas's philosophy on profits. Profits should be the number one focus of any company."

"What?"

"They should be the number one focus of any company."

"But that seems like it goes against his whole fulfilled-people focus you talked about."

"Not at all. Without profits the company can't function. If the company can't function, no one can get paid. And if no one can get paid, no matter how fulfilled they are, the people won't be able to stick around very long. Pretty soon you have no people, no products, no customers, and no company. Everyone loses. But if the company is always profitable, then the people can get paid for doing things that fulfill them, the customers are happy, and everyone wins."

"Hmm."

"Let me explain," I said. "If the number one focus is to maximize profits, then the real question is—how to do that? And what Thomas has found is what he explained in the video. You combine talented people who are on a journey towards their own Purpose For Existing with an organization that has a similar PFE. Now you have people in positions where doing their job not only gets them a paycheck, but brings them fulfillment. Then you add in time-tested, proven business models like subscription, advertising, franchise, or whichever one makes the most sense. And examples of those you can find all over the place. Every industry has them, and again, they're already proven to work."

Sonia nodded. "I can see where that would be effective."

"It is, and effectiveness equals profits. You said you wanted numbers, right?"

"I did."

"Can I borrow a piece of paper and a pen?"

Sonia brought out her satchel and handed me a page from her notebook and a pen with a strange-looking parrot on the top.

I looked at the pen and smiled. "What have we got here?"

She smiled back. "I know, it's goofy looking. But every time I look at it I laugh."

"I like it. Okay, you wanted statistics and examples. There are two big factors that impact profits as they relate to people. The first is productivity; how effective people are. The second is attrition; how often are people quitting and therefore needing to be rehired. Which one do you want to talk about first?"

"Which one is more fun to talk about?"

"They're both tremendously entertaining."

Sonia laughed. "Well, in that case, how about productivity first and then attrition as the encore."

"Alright, for the sake of easy math, let's say we have one thousand people in our company, which we will call AverageCo. Our net income for the year—revenue minus expenses—is $200 million. If you average that out, it means each person is currently generating an average of $200,000 in profits each year. You with me so far?"

"Got it. Although I wouldn't say that everyone in a company has an equal impact on profits."

"Agreed, some people's responsibilities are easy to link to profits and have a bigger direct impact. Others aren't so easy to link and have a lesser impact. However, if everyone is working as a collective team on a common journey, and one of the common goals of the team is to maximize the organization's profits, then in truth, everyone is responsible for profits."

Sonia nodded. "Okay, I'll buy that."

"Great. In that case, let's talk about productivity. How productive would you say the average person is at work?"

"How productive are they?"

"Uh-huh. On a scale of one to one hundred, how close are they to being totally dedicated, totally efficient, totally committed to whatever they get paid to do? Another way to look at it is how much time do they waste, versus how much time are they doing everything possible to help the company fulfill its Purpose For Existing. Here, I'll make it easy on you. Take these five questions and put in your answers. We'll assume these each gets equal weighting of twenty percent of the total productivity answer."

I wrote out five questions on the paper Sonia had given me.

Productivity Question	Ranking 1-10 (1 is low productivity, 10 is high)
1. People are enthused when they show up on a Monday morning.	
2. People perform their tasks without someone watching over them. They don't try to get out of doing what they are supposed to be doing. (Ex., excessive social discussions, lunch breaks, wandering the halls-.-.-.-)	
3. People understand the PFE of the organization (could be department, division, etc., depending on the level of leader doing the assessment).	
4. People understand how what they do helps the organization fulfill its PFE.	
5. People are fulfilling their own PFE through the job they get paid to do. (If you don't think people understand their own PFE, this gets a 1.)	
Total	

"Okay," I said, and handed the paper to her. "Go ahead and fill those in. One is the low end of the scale, and ten is the high end. So for example, with the first question—people are enthused when they show up on a Monday morning—a one would indicate not enthused at all, and a ten would indicate they are extremely enthused. Then take the total number at the bottom and multiply by two. That gives us an easy way to figure out productivity on a scale of one to one hundred."

I waited a few moments while Sonia filled in her answers. "What did you come up with?"

She ran her finger down the answers on her sheet. "I had six for the first question, seven for the second, seven for the third, eight for the fourth, and six for the fifth. So then I add that up and multiply by two . . ." She looked up at me. "Sixty-eight. Is that right?"

I smiled. "Perfect. Actually though, there really is no right or wrong. It's just whatever you think the number is for where you work, or in our example, the average person in our average company."

"So now what?"

"Well, now we go back to our initial observations about our average company. We already figured out each employee generates $200,000 per year toward the total net income. And based on what you just figured out, they generate that working at sixty-eight percent productivity. Here's where Thomas has made a lot of money in his companies. Right from the start, Thomas figured out when people get paid to do things that fulfill them, versus get paid to do things that don't fulfill them, they are more productive. Not surprising, right? If you look at those questions, it's pretty easy to see how the numbers would go up if the average person was spending their time on something that fulfilled them in some way.

"But here's the big aha! Let's say the sixty-eight percent you figured out went up to just eighty percent. Well, at sixty-eight percent each employee generated $200,000 toward net income. We do some basic algebra . . ." I wrote out the formula on Sonia's paper.

$$\frac{68}{200{,}000} = \frac{80}{X}$$

$$X = \frac{(80)\,(200{,}000)}{68}$$

$$X = 235{,}294$$

"And we see that at eighty percent productivity, those same employees now generate over \$235,294 per person per year. Which means since AverageCo has one thousand employees, the company just increased their net income by—"

"Over \$35 million," Sonia said.

"Correct. And that's not revenue, that's profit. *A lot* of profit."

Sonia took the piece of paper I had been writing on and looked at it. "So how do you go from sixty-eight to eighty percent productivity?"

"Good question," I responded. "Hold that thought because I want to show you the other area I mentioned. Remember I said productivity is one opportunity, and the second is attrition. Attrition rates vary a lot by industry. Professional consulting might be around fifteen percent. Something like call-center work could be as high as forty-five percent. For our example, let's assign something in the midrange for our average company. How does twenty-four percent work for you?"

"Sounds good."

"Okay, so here is where Thomas's companies make a significant contribution to their total profit. At a twenty-four percent attrition rate, that means 240 people leave AverageCo each year. Now in most companies, that doesn't get a lot of attention. Why?"

Sonia looked at me. "Honestly? First of all, people are used to it. If that's about the amount of people who usually leave the company, then when they leave, no one really notices. Secondly, it doesn't get a lot of attention because the expenses typically come out of the Human Resource budget, and in most companies, people don't look at Human Resources as a contributor towards the overall company profitability."

I smiled. "I agree. As a matter of fact I've had executives at all levels tell me when someone quits and they're a person short, that isn't so bad because it keeps that salary money in their budget. They're not so happy when I explain to them what I'm about to explain to you. What are the costs each time someone leaves AverageCo and a new person has to be brought in?"

Sonia put her hand on her chin. "Well, it varies company by company, but in general there's a cost with hiring in a new person. You have to place ads or pay recruiting firms or headhunters. And once you hire someone, there's the cost of training that new person as well."

"You're right, those are certainly two of the costs. And those alone hurt companies a great deal in terms of their profits. But those pale in comparison to the even bigger productivity hits." I looked at her. "How productive do you think someone is for the three months prior to when they leave a job they don't like?"

Sonia laughed. "Do you want me to speak from personal experience, or how productive people should be?"

"Personal experience preferred please."

She laughed again. "Well, I know for myself, and for my friends— and it really doesn't seem to matter what level they are at—once we start looking for a job, and especially once we've locked up another job, everything pretty much goes on cruise control. I'd say it's a downward sliding number as the person gets closer to leaving, but someone who is quitting a job they don't like is probably operating at an average of around fifty percent productivity for the last three months before they leave."

"Okay," I said. "And how about when a new person starts? How productive are they for their *first* three months?"

"Well, again, it probably isn't a steady number and it depends on the complexity of the job. This one probably starts pretty low and then rises a lot by the end of the third month. I'd say a fifty percent productivity average is probably right for this as well."

"Excellent. And before I show you the math, keep in mind one other thing. When customers and suppliers and vendors keep dealing with new people who are operating at less than full productivity, it makes for a bad experience. In general, people do not like change. They especially don't like it if the change means they are going to get subpar assistance and support. When that's what a company keeps offering, those people find someone else to give their money to.

"Okay, here's the math on all this. By the way, the attrition rate in Thomas's company—never more than five percent. So I'll use that as the number for our improved AverageCo."

I wrote out all the information we had talked about, hit the calculator function on my phone and did a couple of quick calculations. Then I filled in the chart I had created.

	Average Co.	Average Co. Improved
Annual Attrition	24%	5%
Stated Productivity	68%	80%
Productivity for people 3 months before departure and for first three months of new people.	50%	50%
Actual productivity when 50% productivity of departing and new people is factored in.	64%	79%
Net income gain due to productivity improvements at 24% attrition rate.		$28,643,246
Additional net income gain due to productivity improvements because of lower attrition rate.		$17,902,010
Net income gain because of lower recruiting and training costs from lower attrition rate.		$4,560,000
Total Net Income Gain		$51,105,276

Sonia looked at the numbers I had written down. "Sorry, Joe, you're going to have to walk me through what you did here."

"No problem. It's a combination of what we just discussed, plus the numbers we used in our original calculation. Remember when I said that as a company the total net income was $200 million, and so with one thousand employees that resulted in a per person contribution to net income of $200,000?"

"I do."

"Excellent. Well, all I did was calculate what kind of a boost the company's net income would get if two things were improved—their overall employee productivity, and their attrition rate. However, I had to factor in something really important."

"The lower productivity of all the people who are leaving and the new people who are coming in," Sonia said.

"Exactly. Instead of producing at sixty-eight percent, which is what we came up with from the questions, or eighty percent, which is our hypothetical new productivity level, in both scenarios all the people leaving are producing at fifty percent for the three months prior to their departure, and all the new people are producing at fifty percent for the first three months of their employment."

Sonia nodded. "I see what you did. And I also see the point you were making. Having a high turnover rate has a more serious negative impact on profits than people realize."

"Correct. Improving general productivity certainly has a big impact on a company's profits. When you combine productivity improvements with lower attrition rates, though, that's when you get the most impact."

"Which brings me back to my earlier question," Sonia asked. "How do you do it?"

"That's where Thomas is a genius. He figured out that the more closely aligned someone's Purpose For Existing is to an organization's Purpose For Existing, the more likely they are to stick around. And the more closely aligned their responsibilities are to both their PFE and Big Five for Life, which I'll explain in a minute, the more productive they are and the more likely they are to stick around.

"The total net effect is since his people stay longer and are more productive, Thomas's company's profits are higher. Like I said before, having profits as the number one focus of his companies isn't counter to Thomas's people strategies, because it's his people strategies that create the profitability.

"I also promised you statistics, didn't I?"

Sonia laughed. "You did."

"For starters, Thomas has been proving this in his companies for two decades. As I said earlier, his attrition rates have never been higher than five percent, and I'd put his productivity numbers in the nineties. If you're looking for some external number, though, a great study just came out. It was profiled in Fortune magazine. A joint study was done by Cornell University and the Gevity Institute in which they looked at the results of over three hundred businesses. They looked at three main components.

"The first was employee fit. Did companies hire someone because their skills matched the tasks the job required, or did they hire someone because they would be a good fit with the company's values and culture?"

"That sounds similar to what you've described about Thomas's policy of a Purpose For Existing fit," Sonia remarked.

I nodded. "It is. The second component the study looked at was leadership and management tactics. Did the leaders closely monitor all aspects of people's jobs, or did they give them flexibility to get the job done in the way they thought was best? Although you and I haven't talked about it, Thomas has always created a culture where good people are hired in and then given the flexibility to find the best ways to achieve success. His belief is if you have to watch people to make sure they're doing what needs to be done, then you've got the wrong people."

"And the third component?" Sonia asked.

"The third was on how companies acquired and retained employees, which is very relevant to the math you and I just completed. They looked to see if the companies motivated people through salaries and other financial drivers, or did they create an atmosphere where people felt like they were part of something? If I remember right, they used the term a 'familylike work environment.' "

"That also sounds similar to Thomas's Purpose For Existing technique," Sonia said. "So what were the results?"

I smiled. "You really are ready for some statistics, aren't you?"

She laughed. "Bring them on."

"I'll give you one set that incorporates all three main components of the study." I smiled. "Mostly because that's the one set I remember. You can find the rest in the magazine or at www .gevityinstitute.com.

"When companies that (a) hired not on job fit, but on how a person would fit with the company's culture, (b) didn't micromanage, but instead gave people greater autonomy and let them manage themselves, and (c) motivated not through money, but by creating the 'familylike' environment, were compared to companies that did the opposite of those three . . ." I paused for dramatic effect.

Sonia looked at me and laughed again. "Yes?"

"They had twenty-two percent higher sales growth, twenty-three percent higher profit growth, and sixty-seven percent lower employee attrition."

Sonia picked up the piece of paper where we had crafted our example. "That's right in line with what we calculated," she said.

"Uh-huh. And you were the one who supplied the key statistic about productivity. You must have been right-on with your answers to those initial productivity questions."

Chapter Eleven

SONIA TOOK THE PIECE OF PAPER WE HAD WRITTEN on and put it in her satchel. "Joe, what you just walked me through is not your normal everyday stuff. How do you know all this?"

I smiled. "Fulfill U."

"Fulfill U?"

"Uh-huh. Twice per year Thomas invites all the new travelers who have joined all his companies, along with his key partners, customers, and suppliers, to a three-day event. The point of the three days is for Thomas and the leaders in his companies to share their philosophies on where their companies are going, why they're going there, and what methods they've found that have been successful in helping them along. Basically, Thomas and his leaders invite the attendees to join them on their respective journeys for a few days."

"Who pays for all of that?"

"Thomas's founding company pays for the whole thing. There were over two thousand people at the last one."

"And you attended it?"

"Actually, I teach it. I come in about four weeks before each one to work on it, then head out a week or two afterwards."

"How did you get that job?"

"Actually it was Thomas's idea. It was the best solution we could come up with for fulfilling my Big Five for Life."

She smiled. "The Big Five for Life? Weren't you supposed to tell me what that meant a little while ago?"

I nodded and smiled back. "I was. Are you ready for another story?"

"Let's hear it."

"Okay, backtrack to the first part of our conversation, when I shared with you about Thomas asking me the museum-day-morning question. After that discussion, Thomas and I began meeting every Monday at the train, and we'd talk during our commute. Sometimes it was about business, other times about life. Just good conversations. The only day I ever saw him was on Mondays.

"Well, a few months into our talks, he and I were on the train and I was griping about heading off to work. He asked me why I did the work I did if I disliked it so much. I thought about his question and I told him I didn't know what else I would do. So he asked me if I wanted to meet someone interesting. Someone who would probably 'change my life for the better' was the way he put it."

Sonia looked at me. "That's a tough offer to refuse."

"It was, and so I didn't. Thomas set up a lunch meeting at, of all places, a zoo."

"A zoo?"

"Uh-huh. On the day of the meeting, Thomas and I met at the entrance to the zoo and he walked me to the state-of-the-art gorilla exhibit they have. When we arrived, a young woman in khaki clothes was standing near the entry doors. She looked to be in her mid to late twenties, and I noticed immediately that just like Thomas, she had incredible presence.

"As soon as we walked up, she gave Thomas a big hug and greeted him."

"GOOD TO SEE you, Thomas."

"Likewise, Katie. How are you?"

"Things are great, absolutely great. You caught me in between trips. I leave for Kenya in about two weeks."

Thomas turned to me. "Katie, I want to introduce you to the friend of mine I mentioned on the phone. This is Joe."

Katie smiled again and shook my hand. "Nice to meet you, Joe. Thomas tells me you hate your work life."

I laughed at her honesty and straightforwardness. "Nice to meet you too." I turned to Thomas. "Thanks for painting me in such a great light."

"Oh, no, he said you were a great guy." Katie winked at Thomas. "Just that you hate your work life."

Thomas laughed. "Well, if I didn't say it, you were sure to find it out for yourself. Joe is a great guy. He's in search mode, though, so I thought perhaps you could tell him your story and maybe give him some inspiration for his own. And if you don't mind, I'm going to leave him in your very capable hands and visit some friends while I'm here."

Katie turned to me. "Is that okay with you?"

I nodded. "Fine by me. Just don't drop me in the lion cage."

She smiled. "Nope, we already did that with two people today. No need for another one."

Thomas laughed. "I see this is going to work out just fine. Joe, I'll see you on the train. Katie, thank you." Then Thomas and Katie hugged, and he walked off.

"He has other friends here at the zoo?" I asked.

"Uh-huh, two in particular who have a tremendous impact on our success. You can meet them later if you want."

"Really, where do they work?"

"Over by the pachyderm house. They're a *big* part of the zoo."

I smiled. "Why do I feel like I'm being set up? Thomas's friends aren't people, are they?"

Katie smiled back. "Well done, Joe. Nope, they aren't people. One of Thomas's companies sponsored the renovation for the elephant area. Two years ago I guided Thomas, his wife, Maggie, and almost thirty of the people who work with him on safari in Africa. We had some fantastic animal experiences, especially with elephants, and so when they came back, they decided to take a percentage of their profits each year and donate them to the zoo.

"Thomas's friends are two little baby elephants and their mothers. They were going to be killed because they kept getting into the local people's farms and eating all the crops. We took them in instead. Thomas visits them every time he's here. So do the people who work with him. I see them often. It's amazing how quickly people begin to feel a part of something when they really care about it and help create it."

I smiled. "From what he's been telling me, that sounds like how Thomas builds his companies."

"Knowing Thomas, it probably is. It's certainly more effective than having people spend their time on activities they don't care about. You should see some of the things people do around here, and they don't even get paid for them."

"Seriously?"

"Oh, yeah. About five years ago we started a volunteer program.

People from around the city who love animals volunteer to spend time at the zoo. They instruct visitors, help with the animals. . . . We started with just a few people and now we have close to a hundred. Think of the impact that has. Because of our volunteers we're able to offer visitors a much deeper experience. That not only helps us fulfill our purpose, but it also brings people back, which results in more money for the zoo. And since the people are volunteers, we don't even have to pay them, which is good, because we couldn't afford to."

I nodded my head. "Impressive."

She smiled. "Thanks, we think so."

I looked beyond Katie into the building she had been standing in front of. "Is this where you work?"

"Only part of the time. I spend close to six months here and the other six months each year overseas. We have a number of joint programs with organizations throughout Africa, so I spend quite a bit of time over there working with them. The idea is for all of us to share information about how best to protect the animals. With the way I split my time I'm able to offer both the perspective from the field and also all the insights we gain by being able to observe the animals up close here at the zoo." Katie motioned toward the entry door. "Would you like a tour?"

"Sure."

For the next thirty minutes, Katie walked me through each of the observation areas and exhibits. It was phenomenal. I couldn't believe how well each piece was put together. It was informative, educational, interesting, entertaining . . . And clearly it was a hit with visitors. There were dozens of moms with strollers and hundreds of little kids.

"This is so much better than the zoos I visited as a kid," I said.

She nodded. "Isn't it? We've come a long way since the days of concrete cells and bars. Thank goodness." She motioned to the different exhibits inside the building. "Thomas was a big factor in all of this you know."

"I didn't know that."

"He was. His technique of an organization focusing on its Purpose For Existing or PFE, was a big driver in making all of this happen. When we started this project, we began by creating that. Then we created our project Big Five for Life. And then every step along the way we constantly checked ourselves against those things to make sure we were on track. For example, take a look at this exhibit."

Katie guided me to a giant glass enclosure. Inside, four gorillas of various ages and sizes were playing on branches. "What do you see?"

"Gorillas."

"Look deeper. Look how their habitat is designed."

I shifted my attention from the animals to the space itself.

"What do you see now?"

I looked at Katie. "Interesting. The animals can go from indoors to outdoors at their preference through the open glass door over there."

She nodded. "Yes, what else?"

"Let's see. The outdoor habitat is real, not artificial. When the gorillas are outside, they're in the midst of actual plants and bugs, and trees. And here in the inside habitat, the bottom of the habitat has wood chips, which I assume is a more realistic representation of their natural environment."

She nodded again. "It is. Anything else?"

I looked at all the little kids gathered at the glass staring at the gorillas. "You lowered the wall. When I used to go to the zoo, my parents had to hold me up so I could see the animals. You designed this so the kids are at eye level with the gorillas."

She smiled. "Exactly. Even the smallest child can see these animals." She touched my arm. "Look at that."

A little girl about two years old was standing at the glass with her hands up on it. On the other side of the glass, a small gorilla was doing the exact same thing. They were nose to nose.

"There's more too," Katie said. "The glass is soundproofed so the animals don't get distracted by the enthusiastic yells of the little ones here. And the transition from the inside habitat to the outside is all glass so people and the gorillas can look out and see real plants and real trees. We designed all of that, and all the educational exhibits here, to fulfill our PFE and Big Five for Life."

Chapter Twelve

SONIA LOOKED AT ME AND SMILED. "NOW I THINK you're just teasing me with this whole Big Five for Life thing, Joe. What is it?"

I laughed. "I'm just to that part of the story."

KATIE AND I sat down on a bench where we could watch the gorillas. Two of the younger ones were wrestling.

"Those little ones remind me of my younger brothers when they were kids," she said. "Only my brothers used to bite more."

I smiled. "Katie, I understand the PFE concept you've mentioned. Thomas has explained that to me a couple of times before. What did you mean with the Big Five for Life, though?"

She turned and gave me a surprised look. "Thomas didn't share that with you yet?"

"No."

She nodded. "Ah, so that's what he had in mind for today. He mentioned you were unhappy at your job, but I just assumed he had shared the Big Five for Life with you. Okay, let me backtrack a bit.

Thomas and I met almost fifteen years ago. He and his wife, Maggie, were volunteer judges for the state science-fair competition. Thomas happened to be the judge for my project, which was on 'The Future of Species—Why it would be more productive for humans and animals to be interactive than in observational isolation.'" She smiled. "I'll save the details of the speech for another conversation.

"When I finished presenting, and the judges had asked all their questions, they all walked away except for Thomas. He told me my presentation was the best he'd heard in three years of judging, and he asked me what I wanted to do with my life. I told him I wasn't sure. I wanted it to be something with animals, but everyone in my family and at school was telling me you couldn't make a decent living dealing with animals. He changed my outlook on life with a single statement."

"What was it?"

"He looked me in the eye and said, 'They're wrong.' He told me he had two women he thought I would be very happy I met. Two women who would 'change my life for the better' was the way he put it."

I smiled.

"What?"

"That's how he described you when he asked if I wanted to meet you. He used those exact words."

Katie nodded. "That's a high compliment considering who he introduced me to. After Thomas mentioned the two women to me, he wrote down the name of my school. And I kid you not, two days later on the Monday after the contest, a FedEx package arrived at my school for me. You should have seen the look on the receptionist's face when I came in to get it. Inside the package were two books.

The first was the life story of Jane Goodall. Do you know who she is?"

"Not exactly. Something with chimpanzees, right?"

"Not just something, she was a pioneer in the field of chimpanzee research and is one of the most recognized experts and spokeswomen in the field. Her story is amazing. She had no formal training, no specific education to prepare her, but because of her tremendous passion, courage, and adventurous spirit, she has lived this amazing life."

"And the second book?"

"The second book was the story of a young man who goes to Africa for no other reason than it's the one thing he finds he has passion about. He saves for two years, and when he arrives, he meets this very old, very wise woman named Ma Ma Gombe, who offers to walk him across the African continent. The story is about their journey together—the dangers they encounter, the animals they see, the people they meet, the lessons she teaches him."

"Wow!" I said.

"Wow indeed. Picture putting those two books, with those two women role models, into the hands of a fifteen-year-old thirsty for inspiration. Maybe I would have eventually gotten to where I am if I'd never met Thomas, and never read those books, but probably not. At a minimum, he certainly helped speed things along."

"So where does the Big Five for Life come into play?"

"Oh, sorry. In the second book, one of the major lessons the Ma Ma Gombe character teaches the young man as they are walking across Africa is about choosing one's own Big Five for Life. See, when people visit Africa and they go on safari, the rangers and guides always talk about the African Big Five. They are the five animals everyone wants to see."

"Which ones are they?"

"Lion, leopard, rhinoceros, elephant, and African buffalo. And people gauge the success of their safari experience on how many of the African Big Five they see. So if they see three of the five species, they consider it an average safari, four would be pretty good, and five would be completely successful.

"What the Ma Ma Gombe character shares, is we have the opportunity to define success for our existence too. We do it by choosing our Big Five for Life. They are the five things we most want to do, see, or experience before we die. The five things *so* important to us, that if we did, saw, or experienced them, then in our last moments—those final seconds before we pass away—we could look back over our life and know it was a success.

"It would be a success as we—and that's the key word there—*we* defined success for ourselves. Because no matter what else we did or didn't get to, we got to our Big Five for Life.

"Thomas has taken this concept to all kinds of different levels in his companies. For example, before they can get hired, each prospective person has to articulate not only how their personal Purpose For Existing is a fit with the companies, but also what their Big Five for Life are. Then they and the person hiring them sit down and talk about the ways in which the person can fulfill their Big Five for Life by performing the job they are being hired to do. If there's no fit, then the person doesn't get hired.

"That's one of the ways Thomas makes sure his employees are motivated. How motivated would you be at work if you got paid to fulfill the five things that if you did, saw, or experienced them, you could say on your deathbed that your life was a success?"

I nodded. "Very motivated."

"Exactly. And as Thomas will tell you, motivated people are more productive, and more productive people mean happier customers, and that means higher profits. Everybody wins."

"Hard to fathom," I said.

Katie looked up at me. "Only when you're in a company that's nothing like it. For Thomas's people it's hard to fathom doing it any other way. Each person has their Big Five for Life on their desk along with links showing how those Big Five for Life are tied to what the person does every day. And it's a huge part of their culture. Thomas and all of his leaders have regular discussions with their teams to make sure the people's roles in the company are still linked to their Big Five for Life. And when they aren't, then they jointly figure out some new roles. Those types of discussions happen at all levels in the organization."

I looked around at the exhibit. "So you've adopted something similar here?"

"Actually *copied* would be more accurate. With Thomas's approval and the advice of both him and a bunch of his people who helped us, we use the same technique for interviewing and ongoing evaluation to see what's working and what's not. We also use the same technique for projects, which is actually what I was referring to when we first got on the Big Five for Life topic."

"What's the technique for projects?"

"Well, in our case, we figured out our PFE—Purpose For Existing—for this new exhibit. Why was it going to exist in the first place? Then we figured out what success would mean from the standpoint of the Big Five for Life. What did we want to achieve by creating this exhibit? What were the five things we wanted our visitors to do, see, and experience, which in our case included take away, from their visit here?

"That way, as we came up with ideas and began to make the

exhibit a reality, it was easy to test whether we were on the path to success. Thomas has a funny analogy he uses. Have you ever watched any of those late night comedy talk shows?"

"Sure, where the hosts do all kinds of crazy things and interview celebrities?"

"Exactly. On one of those shows, the host used to do this skit where he would get dressed up in a Velcro suit. Then he would take a running start and jump off a trampoline onto a Velcro wall. When his body would hit the wall, the Velcro would all catch, and the host would stick to the wall."

I laughed. "I remember that."

"That's how Thomas describes the Purpose For Existing and Big Five for Life. They are the Velcro wall of success. As you come up with ideas, and models, and prototypes, you constantly throw them up against your Velcro wall. If they meet your PFE and Big Five for Life, then they will stick, and you use them. If they don't, then to use them would be foolish. They wouldn't lead to success as you've defined success. I love using it with my teams because it gives everyone the same common criteria to evaluate things. It also gives us all a common language. That way we're always all on the same page, so we're way more productive than we used to be."

"That seems so simple," I said.

She nodded. "It is and it isn't. At the start of a project it's actually easier to just start doing a bunch of stuff than it is to really sit down and define success—create your Velcro wall. But it comes back to haunt you pretty quick as you start to get into it. You end up with people going off in ten different directions because they all have their own idea of what success looks like. And often the results are a disaster.

"How many projects have you seen where by the time people

are done, the results don't even fulfill the need first described in the project proposal?"

"A lot."

"Think of all the time and money wasted on those. Not to mention that the end product is useless. So in addition to all the time and money that went into creating the result, you're no better off than when you started. When you think about it in those terms, there's no comparison to investing some effort up front to create the Velcro wall of your PFE and Big Five for Life."

Katie stopped talking and turned to look at me. She was looking into my eyes. She stared into them to the point I started to feel a little uncomfortable.

"I don't see tremendous joy there, Joe," she finally said. "I'm not one to tell anyone else how they should live their life. I'm also not one to let an opportunity pass me by when I can try to return the favor Thomas did me when he sent me those two books. I don't think you know what your personal Purpose For Existing and Big Five for Life are. I don't think you have a Velcro wall to bounce options off of.

"And I have a hunch if you figure out what your PFE and Big Five for Life are, and then you look at your schedule for next week and circle all the items, all the meetings, all the activities that will help you fulfill them—I don't think there will be too many circles. And there's a big danger with that, Joe. Because a week turns into a month, a month into a year, and before you know it, you're at the very end. If there aren't many circles for next week, there probably won't be too many circles ever. And that means at the end—in your own eyes—your life won't have been a success."

Katie held her gaze for a few seconds more and I looked away.

"Sorry," she said. "I know that may not be easy to hear. Thomas introduced us for a reason. I don't know exactly why. Maybe it's because we're similar in age, or because he thinks we have some of the same interests. But I think maybe he introduced us because he wanted you to hear that from me."

Chapter Thirteen

WHEN I COMPLETED THE STORY, I LOOKED AT sonia. she was silent.

"Okay," she began, "I'm sure you're tired of hearing it, but wow. Wow!"

I laughed. "Yeah, it was a 'Wow!' type meeting."

"Katie was lucky to meet Thomas. You were lucky to meet both of them."

"Without a doubt. And I've learned from Thomas, when you have the opportunity to meet amazing people and establish friendships with them, don't let the opportunity pass by. Thomas teaches all his people that one of the reasons he has achieved the financial and personal success he has is because he surrounds himself with winners. People who are winning their own personal game of life. And in part, that's how he has created such successful companies. He builds them with winners. He inspires his people, and they in turn inspire him."

"So do you keep in touch with Katie?"

"I do."

"Is she still going back and forth to Africa?"

"Yes, she is. She's so locked onto her personal Purpose For Existing and Big Five for Life there's rarely a moment of indecision in her life. And because of that she has about as little stress as anyone I've ever met. There's no second-guessing things for Katie. If it supports her PFE and Big Five for Life, she does it. If it doesn't, she doesn't."

Sonia smiled. "How about you?"

"Well, as you can imagine, that was a big day—a big meeting—for me. It wasn't just the concept. I think if I had heard the concept from someone who wasn't living it, or who didn't have Katie's intensity, I would have been impressed and intrigued, but I probably would have forgotten it. But seeing her in her element at the zoo and seeing the great work she and her team had done brought it closer to home. Then when she called me out at the end of our conversation . . . that was a wake-up call for me.

"So I spoke with Thomas about it, and he was kind enough to help me craft out my Purpose For Existing and Big Five for Life. Now I live them. Lots of circles on my calendar now." I smiled.

Chapter Fourteen

"LADIES AND GENTLEMEN, FLIGHT 847 FROM barcelona to Chicago is now making its initial descent. Please secure all tray tables and put all seats in their upright and locked position."

I blinked my eyes a few times and glanced at my watch. It was 8:30 a.m. Chicago time. I looked at Sonia, but she was still sleeping. We had talked for a good portion of the flight and had then both decided to try to get some rest. I stretched my arms over my head and rolled my shoulders to try to loosen the stiffness.

"Looks like we're almost there." It was Sonia.

"I think so."

She smiled. "Thanks for the great discussions, Joe. I hope your friend Thomas recovers. He sounds like a great guy."

"Thanks, I hope so too."

I reached into my backpack and pulled out one of my cards. "Here's my contact information. Let's stay in touch."

She took the card, read it, then turned it over. "Hey, these are your Big Five for Life and PFE."

"Uh-huh. Everyone who works with Thomas has them on the back of their cards. It's a great reminder of why we do what we do, and it certainly sets us apart when we meet people. They always ask what it means, and it gets you into some memorable discussions."

JOE POGRETE
My PFE & Big Five for Life

PFE: To experience all that I want out of life, so that I live with no regrets.

BFFL:

B — Be traveling the world for at least six months per year.

W — Write a song that breaks the top ten of the pop charts.

I — Inspire people through my writings, presentations, and by being who I am. Make a difference.

S — Speak Spanish fluently.

E — Exercise my mind and body daily, so that I'm always growing.

If you or someone you know can help me fulfill any of these, please contact me at:
www.mybigfive.com/pogrete

Sonia read through the items on my card:

"Interesting," she said. "Why do you have BWISE on the left?"

"It's just a little acronym I created when I first came up with my list, to help me remember my Big Five for Life. That's another Thomas idea. I've seen some really fun ones people have created. One guy has BEBIG, so every day he looks at what he has planned and asks himself, if he does those things, will he BEBIG? Another woman uses GREAT for hers. So, is today a GREAT day?"

Sonia laughed, "Well, BWISE certainly describes you today, Joe. You inspired me with your stories about Thomas and Katie. I'm going to think about my own Big Five for Life and see how many circles I've got on my calendar for next week." She handed me one of her cards. "Nothing exotic about this. Although there will be the next time I see you. I like that idea."

She pulled out another of her cards and on the back wrote:

My PFE & Big Five for Life
_____

PFE:
BFFL:
#1 –
#2 –
#3 –
#4 –
#5 –

AFTER CLAIMING my bags I walked outside and got into the cab line.

I wish I were back under different circumstances, I thought. It was fun speaking with Sonia about Thomas and what he had taught me. It was fun to share his teachings with others. It wasn't fun to face the reality that something was really wrong with him . . . that he was dying.

I checked my messages during the cab ride into the city. Maggie had left me one the night before during the flight. "Joe, Thomas is in the hospital again. He's going for some tests, and they've already told him he'll have to stay the night. When you land, come by here if you can."

"Change of plans," I told the cabdriver. "Northwestern Memorial Hospital please."

The thought of the hospital, and of Thomas's life being taken from him, reminded me of my friend Clark. Clark was the CEO at one of Thomas's subsidiary companies. I had been introduced to Clark through Dawn, his VP of operations. She and I had known each other for years, and now all of us were good friends. One of Clark's favorite expressions when he sensed pressure or stress among his people was "We're not saving lives here." For some reason, sitting there in the cab and thinking of Thomas, the thought occurred to me that Thomas, and all who worked with him and made the Big Five for Life a requirement for their people, really were saving lives. And that included Clark and Dawn.

If leaders weren't helping their people fulfill their Big Five for Life, then what were they really doing? Basically they were taking people's lives in exchange for money. It was a harsh assessment and not one I thought most people would feel comfortable with. How many leaders would want to reflect on their own life and realize they could have made a lot of money by helping fulfill a lot of lives, and instead they made a lot of money by using a lot of lives? *Perhaps a little too harsh*, I thought to myself. *But somewhere in there is a lot of truth.*

Chapter Fifteen

"SOME PEOPLE WILL DO ANYTHING FOR A LITTLE attention," I said as I walked into Thomas's hospital room. I had caught Maggie's eye through the window while I was standing outside the room and she'd waved for me to come in. Thomas was lying in a bed that faced the wall. His head and back were slightly inclined.

"And some people will do anything in the hopes of getting a date, like fleeing the country and heading to Spain," a voice replied back. It was Thomas.

"They don't know I work with Thomas Derale over there," I replied. "It improves my chances."

Thomas chuckled and reached his hand out to me. "How are you, Joe? How was Spain?"

I held his arm and grasped his shoulder with my other hand. "Good. Why don't you stop playing the sympathy angle here and you and Maggie and I can catch the next flight to Barcelona. We'll do a little backpacking down the coast. The two of you can both help me find a date."

"Impossible," Thomas replied.

This time I chuckled. Thomas reached for a cup of water on the nightstand near his bed, and as he did, I took a good look at him. He had aged a lot since I'd last seen him four months earlier. Maggie stood up from the bed and gave me a warm hug. "Thanks for coming back, Joe."

I put my arms around her and squeezed her tight. "Do you want me to pull him out of there and shake him up a little, or should I let him keep pretending a little longer?" I asked her loudly enough that Thomas could hear.

In reality, I was the one pretending. When I'd first called from Spain, Maggie told me the seriousness of Thomas's condition. A few months earlier he had begun to experience severe headaches, and one time his vision became impaired for almost a full day. After a week of trying over-the-counter medications, the headaches hadn't gone away, so he went to his personal doctor.

They noticed his reflexes were slower than they had been previously, so they sent him to a specialist. Initially the doctors couldn't find anything wrong. His MRI looked normal, and under prescription-strength medicines the headaches had gone away. They recommended he take it easy for a few days and then come back for some additional tests.

As soon as he stopped taking the pain medication, the headaches returned. So he came back to the hospital. This time they injected dye into his bloodstream and allowed it to flow to his brain. Then they did a CAT scan to see what had happened to the dye. Healthy brain tissue absorbs less dye than unhealthy brain tissue. The CAT scan showed a significant mass in his occipital lobe that had absorbed more dye than the rest. That's because it wasn't healthy tissue. It was a large tumor.

In the week that followed, Thomas underwent more tests, and more scans. They tested his reflexes and memory and motor skills. Then on a Tuesday morning, Thomas and Maggie received a call asking them to come to the hospital. Their own physician was there along with the specialist. The doctors explained that the tumor was inoperable. It had grown so large it had spread to the cerebellum and was now twisted around Thomas's brain stem. Because of its size and location, radiation and chemotherapy were also not viable treatment options. In essence . . . there were no options. Thomas was dying.

When Thomas asked how long he had before the disease shut him down completely, they said they didn't know exactly. Two months they thought. Maybe a little more. Maybe less. No one could say for sure.

That was when Maggie had called me. Now here we were.

There would be no pulling Thomas up and shaking him back to health. There would be no backpacking trip for all of us down the coast of Spain. I knew it . . . we all knew it. But I didn't know what else to say.

I released Maggie from our hug and she reached out and squeezed Thomas's hand. "I'm going to see if they will discharge you now that Joe is here to lend a hand at the house."

When the door had closed behind her, I turned to Thomas and put my arm on his shoulder again. "My friend, when I left on my trip, this isn't the type of location I expected us to have our next conversation in." I nodded toward the door. "How's Maggie doing? How are you doing?"

"She's holding it together. We both are." He paused and stared off into space for a few moments. "We've exhausted all the possible options, now things just are what they are. I'm dying, Joe. I didn't even want to come back to the hospital, but one of the medications wasn't working for me and they had to run a test last night to see why."

"What can I do, Thomas? How can I help?"

He smiled. "Well, for starters, thanks for coming back. It's good to see you. Besides that, why don't you stay at the house with us for a while? It would give us all a chance to hang out, talk, catch up . . ."

Say good-bye, I thought to myself.

"And I might need a hand with some things. There are a few loops I want to close before this is over. I realize that may sound foolish, but it would mean a lot to me."

I nodded. "Sure, Thomas," I said softly.

"And another thing." He smiled. "The way you came in here is the way I want it to be until it's over. We've had a lot of laughs over the years, Joe. I don't want it to end with anything that resembles a pity party. Maggie and I already made that agreement. I'd like us to make it too."

I nodded again. "You've got a deal." I forced a smile onto my face and said with as much genuine enthusiasm as I could generate, "In that case, you've got to quit all this screwing around, Thomas. It's almost noon and you're still in bed."

Chapter Sixteen

WHILE WE WAITED FOR MAGGIE TO OBTAIN thomas's release from the hospital, I told him about my trip to Spain, including the plane flight back and my conversations with Sonia. I've always been amazed at how with close friends you can be away from each other for months, even years, and as soon as you're back together, you pick up as if you'd just seen each other the day before. That's how it was with Thomas.

"Did you share with her how upset you got when I told you to tell your boss he was an idiot?" he asked me.

I started laughing. "No, actually I'd forgotten about that." Thomas had shared that advice with me one morning after he'd seen me standing on the train platform and yelling into my cell phone. When we boarded the train, I'd explained to him my boss was an idiot and was always micromanaging me.

"IS THAT because he chooses to be an idiot, or because he doesn't know any other way to lead?" Thomas asked me. "Have you told him he's an idiot? If not, maybe you should."

"Have I what?"

"It takes two to tango, Joe. While *idiot* probably isn't the exact term you should use, the truth is that it's one thing if you call him on it and then he doesn't change. At that point it's your problem, and you either need to leave or quit whining. It's something very different, however, if he just doesn't know.

"I tell my people all the time to make me better. If they read something interesting, tell me. If they want to receive feedback differently, tell me. When they do well, I win, plain and simple. If I seriously disagree with the way they're doing something because it violates my core ethics, or for some other reason, I tell them. Otherwise, I let them play the game the way they can best play it.

"Do you ever watch football, Joe? Imagine a coach recruiting a star quarterback to the team and then making him throw with his opposite hand, just to please the coach. Find out if your boss knows anything about football. And if he does, tell him he's making you throw left-handed, and you're a star when you throw righty. Tell him to let you throw righty for one month, and if the overall results aren't better, you'll go back to his way. And if he won't agree to that, and he won't tell you why, or it's just an ego thing, then leave. How far can you really go in your career with that kind of person as your boss?"

"What if he doesn't know anything about football?"

"Find out what he does know something about and use that as your example."

I BLINKED my eyes a few times and snapped out of the memory.

"I wonder what ever became of that guy," I said to Thomas.

"Which guy?"

"The one you suggested I tell he was an idiot. He really was a terrible leader. Great sales guy, but terrible leader. They should have just let him do his thing as an independent salesperson."

"Or taught him something about leadership before he was made a leader," Thomas said. "His was a classic 'longevity equals leadership' promotion, wasn't it? How many times did you see that in the early part of your career?"

"Too many. You're right. He got zero coaching on leadership. One day he was a sales guy with a big region and the next he was a director leading sixty people who were his peers the day before. And the expectation was he could manage them well. I have to say, you do a great job of not creating that problem in your companies, Thomas."

"That's good. Like you, I'd seen a lot of it, so I made a real effort to let people throw with their right hand if they were right-handed. I made sure that was part of our culture. Some people don't want to be leaders. Why promote them into a position and lifestyle they don't want? And why create a system where if they don't take the promotion, they are looked down upon? All you end up with is unhappy people working for unhappy leaders, and low, low productivity.

"And in the other circumstance, where someone expressed an interest in taking a leadership position, or I thought they had real leadership potential and they were open to trying it, I made sure they were groomed for the role long before the day they were promoted."

I gazed out the window of Thomas's hospital room. "Thomas, why is it you get it?"

"Get what?"

"You understand what it takes to be a great leader."

He looked at me. "Why do you get it?"

"I learned it from you."

He laughed. "That's flattering. I think I've told you before though, Joe, I had some defining moments early in my career that shaped me. Some defining people too. That's a rather complicated story though, let's save that one for another day."

I wanted to tell him we were running out of other days. That I wanted to hear every story of his I hadn't yet heard, before we ran out of time.

It was his time that was running out though. I let it pass. "Thomas, I used one of your stories at the seminar I spoke at in Spain."

"Did you give me credit?"

"Of course not."

Thomas smiled. "Excellent, then I've still got plausible deniability. Which story?"

"The one where you were at the executive retreat and the senior VP said he liked to have his direct reports competing with each other."

Thomas nodded. "I have an enhancement to that story now. I came up with it a couple of months ago."

"What is it?"

"Do you want the full version so you can use it next time?"

"Sure." I sat back in my chair and watched Thomas move up in the bed, trying to make himself more comfortable. *He should be on a stage in front of thousands of people,* I thought to myself, *like I've seen him so many times before. Not sitting in a little hospital bed. This isn't right. It isn't fair.*

Thomas looked at me. "Are you with me?"

"Yeah, sorry, go ahead."

He shook his head in mock disappointment. "Who's the sick one here? Okay, picture yourself on a big stage in front of a large crowd.

The topic of the presentation is 'What is great leadership?' And the answer is—great leadership is like growing a thriving group of fruit-producing papaya trees."

"Papaya trees?"

"Papaya trees. Great leadership is like growing a thriving group of fruit-producing papaya trees."

Thomas began telling his story as if, as he had described, he were up on a stage and there were thousands of people in the audience.

"When you start the process of growing a thriving group of fruit-producing papaya trees, you take hundreds of papaya seeds, and you plant them in a bucket full of fertile ground. Not the bad soil, but the good stuff, the stuff that's full of nutrients and vitamins. And every few days after you've planted the seeds, you water the soil, because you know that with nourishment, some of those little seeds will eventually sprout. You don't step on the seeds, belittle the seeds, or treat them poorly. You don't smash the dirt they're in. You give them every opportunity, because you want them to sprout, to grow, to become strong papaya trees that bear fruit.

"In a few weeks, lo and behold, you start to see sprouts. Your efforts are paying off. Partly it's because of what you've done. Partly it's because of what you haven't done that would have been detrimental to the seeds. And partly it's because of the pure potential that lives within every seed, regardless of what you do.

"A few weeks go by and you look at your bucket and realize the sprouts have actually become plants. There are lots of them, dozens, maybe even a hundred, all slowly growing into papaya trees. At this point, they are all still about the same size, just a couple of inches tall.

"Over the next couple of weeks, you begin to notice something. It seems some of the plants are beginning to grow faster than the others. When you look closely, you realize what's happening is the plants are starting to compete with each other for light and water. The ones with slightly larger leaves are not only receiving the most sun and nourishment, but they are also keeping those things from the other plants close to them. And as they do that, it appears they are growing faster.

"Left alone, something interesting happens. The plants will grow to a certain size, perhaps a foot and a half to two feet tall for the larger ones. Along the way, about a quarter of the smaller plants, the ones who couldn't get sun and now can't compete for water because they don't have the same lengthy root structure as the others, will die. And if nothing is done at that point, the remaining plants will stop growing.

"See, within the bucket there is limited space to expand, and the plants somehow know this. So they stop growing taller. Over time a few will develop larger leaves than the others and dominate the sun. Because of that, most of the other plants will slowly succumb.

"So at the end of all your efforts, you have a small group of under-sized papaya plants and no fruit to show for it.

"But with just a little effort, and a few different decisions along the way, that end result can be dramatically different. For example, when the plants are about a foot high and still growing, don't leave them all in one bucket. Instead take four or five at a time and put them in new buckets. What you find when you do that, is they *all* keep growing. Sure it happens the occasional papaya plant doesn't make it for one reason or another, but in general, they all keep growing.

"Now this takes a little work, doesn't it? You have to take the time to provide each of those little groups of plants with a new bucket, and with fresh, nutrient-rich soil. But when you do that, you get closer to your goal of fruit-producing papaya trees.

"After another month has gone by, you look at your twenty or so buckets of papaya plants, and you see each bucket doesn't have little plants anymore. Instead, those plants have become little trees. They aren't full grown yet, but they aren't just little plants anymore either. Most of them are now about two and a half to three feet high, and you can tell once again, they are starting to compete with each other. Left alone, one tree in each bucket will begin to dominate, and the others will eventually stop growing, or succumb.

"And so you take each of those little trees in the buckets and you plant them in the ground. They're outside the security of their little buckets, but they now have access to all the earth has to offer. Their roots can grow as deep as they want. Their leaves can grow big and broad because there is unlimited access to the sun, and they can grow tall.

"Now there is an interesting thing that happens when you plant these three-foot papaya trees. If you plant them all by themselves, totally off on their own, they will grow big and tall and have broad leaves, but they will never produce fruit. However, if you plant a few of them together, not so close they block each other, but within a few feet, they will pollinate each other, shade each other depending on the angle of the sun, drop rain from their own leaves onto the leaves of their neighbor when it rains, and because of all of that, they will produce fruit—lots of fruit.

"When they are planted that way, they no longer compete. They exist in a state of synergy. Their presence is an asset to each other's success, not a detriment. And the result of all your efforts is not just a few non-fruit-producing, stunted papaya trees like it might have been. But instead, you have a grove of papaya trees. Dozens upon dozens of them, all producing fruit. Fruit which eventually will create seeds which will grow into even more papaya trees."

At this point, Thomas shifted to the story I had alluded to earlier.

"A few years ago, I was asked to host a leadership summit. Executives from companies all over the world came to share ideas, to learn from each other. And I recall one session in particular I was hosting. In that session, a senior vice president from a huge entertainment company, a company everyone in this room would know if I said their name, shared with the group what he did as a leader to promote successful results was he encouraged competition among his people. He felt the competition made them grow and made them work harder. This was a man who had twenty direct reports, all vice presidents and directors, and who in total had probably two thousand people under him.

"When we took a break, I introduced myself to one of that senior VP's direct reports, a VP who had been quiet during most of our morning session. I asked him what he thought of the leadership summit, and then I asked him what he thought of his leader's comments. He told me the reality was—the competitive environment created by the senior VP was terrible.

"Executives kept critical information from each other so they could make their individual results better. Good employees weren't being promoted because the promotions would mean they would transfer into another person's area, and the executives saw that as a competitive disadvantage. Not only would they lose a good employee, but their competitor would gain one—one who had tremendous knowledge they would share with their new team. He said since they were such a dominant player in their industry, they had no one to fight, so they fought against themselves."

Thomas paused.

"The senior VP was leaving all his papaya plants in one little bucket. He was creating competition, not growing a grove of fruit-producing papaya trees.

"I watched what happened with that company and stayed in contact with the VP. Within two years, many of the best people jumped ship and went to a growing competitor across town. Within two years after that, the market dominance the company had enjoyed was eroding quickly, and the VP himself left. When I talked with him and asked why he had decided to leave now, he told me despite all the signs, the culture hadn't changed. People were still competing with each other. Only now, they were competing to see who could blame someone else for the growth of the competitor. Or who could capitalize because one of their peers was taking a hit and therefore they could make themselves appear that much better."

Thomas paused again, for emphasis.

"Our people are like papaya seeds. The question we need to ask ourselves as leaders is, what are we trying to create? If we want to create a grove of strong, productive leaders who not only produce fruit, but who in the process create new leaders of their own, then we need to nurture them.

"We need to give them opportunities rich with potential, not barren desert. We need to make sure we create an environment where they are growing, not one that stunts their growth through internal competition. We need to give them space to expand, not restrict them so their enthusiasm withers and dies. And when the time is right, we need to take them out of the bucket where they grew up and give them the chance to grow on their own.

"However, when that time comes, we don't put them out somewhere in isolation, out in a vacuum. We do it in the way that best generates fruit—by providing them with an environment where they and other leaders pollinate each other, protect each other, water each other. We do it in a way where they can work together to fulfill their true full potential.

"Ladies and gentleman, as leaders, those are the things we need to do for our people. Because those are the things that make great leaders great."

I sat and looked at Thomas. I felt like applauding. I did applaud. "That was perfect, Thomas. I mean just perfect. Where did you come up with it?"

He smiled. "Well, the part about the senior VP you've heard before. You know that really happened. The rest came to me a few months ago while I was trying to grow a papaya tree in my greenhouse. I just watched what happened at each step along the way, and it struck me how much there was to learn from it. So I wrote a piece about it. I figured I'd give it as a speech at some point. I was planning on a slightly larger audience than just one though." He chuckled.

I nodded enthusiastically. "You should give it to a larger audience. I mean that was really great. What about the next executive retreat in . . ." My words hung in the air. The executive retreat was four months away. Thomas and I both knew he wouldn't be alive then. For just a few moments as I'd listened to him give the speech, I had forgotten where I was and why.

"Sorry, Thomas . . . ," I began, in a solemn voice.

He smiled. "None of that, Joe. You and I made an agreement, remember? You give the speech at the retreat. You'll be great with it."

Chapter Seventeen

I CAME DOWN THE STAIRS. IT WAS EARLY, STILL A little before 7:00 a.m. I hadn't been able to sleep. I'd stayed with Thomas and Maggie many times before, and it had always been constant laughter. The reality of why I was in their house this time kept weighing on me. This wasn't just a social visit, or the prelude to an adventure vacation somewhere.

When I came through the kitchen, I was surprised to see Thomas and Maggie sitting on the patio. They were holding hands and laughing. I turned to go back upstairs and give them some privacy, but as I turned, I heard Maggie call, "It's okay, Joe, come on out and join us."

I walked onto the patio and admired the beautiful view. Their backyard had colorful flowers spaced throughout, and numerous old, giant oak trees. Where their yard ended, a forest began. "I love it out here," I said. "It's so peaceful."

Maggie turned to me. "That was one of the main reasons we bought this place. On our second visit here, there were deer walking in the backyard, and that pretty much sealed the deal for us."

I patted Thomas on the shoulder. "You're up rather early."

"I know. I pretty much power nap my way through the day now. You missed saying hello to Josephine this morning, Joe."

"Josephine? Your Director of First Impressions?"

"Uh-huh. She was dropping these off." He handed me a wicker basket full of blueberry muffins.

"Wow, these look good."

"I'm only on my third one, so I haven't decided yet," Thomas replied.

Maggie took one of the muffins from the basket. "Ever since Thomas told Josephine the news about his diagnosis, she's been here three mornings a week with homemade baked goods. She's also coordinating all the dinner drop-offs. We had so many people bringing meals over it was just going to waste."

"Who was bringing the food?" I asked.

"The people in Thomas's companies."

I mulled that over. It was pretty amazing, really. Thomas was not a poor man by any stretch. In fact, he was wealthy by most standards. Yet here were the people who worked in his companies sending him home-cooked dinners.

Thomas put down his napkin and reached for another muffin. "Josephine says hello, Joe. I told her you were here and she asked me to make sure I kidded you about the first time you came to see me at the office."

"I will never live that down, will I?"

"Live what down?" Maggie asked. "How do I not know this story?"

Thomas looked at me. "Why don't you tell it from your perspective."

I leaned back in my chair and looked at Maggie. "Okay. You know Thomas and I met when he hit me with his museum question on the train platform, right?"

"I do know that."

"Well, Thomas and I had been meeting on the train for a few weeks and having some great discussions on business and life. We were becoming friends really. You know when you make that transition from someone who is more of an acquaintance to someone who you'd call a friend? So one morning—after, as I recall it, I was complaining yet again about my job and boss—Thomas suggested we meet at his office for lunch."

I looked at Thomas. "I think you told me you wanted me to get a good look at the other side, or something like that, wasn't it?"

"Glad to know my words had such small meaning for you, Joe," Thomas kidded, and smiled. "Actually what I told you was I thought your view of work was getting tainted and you needed something that would give you an alternate perspective."

"Okay, I needed an alternate perspective. So he left it at 'why don't you spring a couple of hours on your calendar this Friday and meet me where I work and we'll grab lunch.' Well, Friday rolls around and I head off to the address he gave me, and when I enter the lobby, there's Josephine. And she has this nameplate on her desk that says 'Director of First Impressions,' which I thought was pretty cool. So I walk up to her and explain that I'm there to see Thomas Derale, but I don't even know which department he works in. And she gives me this strange look and says, 'Pardon me, sir?'

"So I explained again that I was there to see Thomas Derale, but I didn't know which department he worked in. And she said, 'Thomas Derale?' Well, the conversation was starting to seem pretty strange, and I remember thinking maybe I was in the wrong place, so I said, 'Yes, Thomas Derale. Does he work here?' And Josephine looks at me and says, 'Sort of, sir. He owns this building. He's the founder, president, and chairman of the board of this company. Are you sure you're here to see Thomas Derale?' "

I turned to Maggie. "Honestly, at that moment the reality was I wasn't so sure."

Maggie started laughing. "You did that to him?" she asked, and poked Thomas.

"I'm telling you, Maggie, I'm so glad there isn't video footage of me at that moment," I said. "I'm sure the look on my face was priceless. You could have blown me over with a hair dryer. And that wasn't the end of the conversation. Keep in mind I still didn't know what Thomas did back then, or anything about his company. So I asked Josephine, 'How many people work here?' Well, by then she must have been thinking I was nuts. She looked at me and asked, 'You mean in this building, or in all of Thomas's companies sir?'

" 'All of them?'

" 'Yes, sir, there are fourteen companies.'

" 'How many people work in all of them?'

" 'Over twelve thousand people, sir. Most of them are here in Chicago, but we also have companies in locations around the globe.' "

"What happened next?" Maggie asked.

"Well, to Josephine's credit, she didn't kick me out like the crazy person I probably seemed like. She called up to Thomas's office and let them know I was there."

Thomas turned to me. "That's why she's a great Director of First Impressions."

"Did you give her that title, or did she pick it?" Maggie asked.

"I did. I told her she could pick what she wanted, but in my mind, like for Joe, she was the first impression many people would have of the company. I explained to her how I had seen multimillion-dollar deals get lost because when people called a company they couldn't get through to the right person, or they weren't treated well, and I never wanted that to happen in my company."

"Is that true about the million-dollar deals?" I asked.

"It is. Early in my career we were looking to do a joint venture with providers of a new scanning technology, and I was very hands-on with the project. Out of the eight companies I called, three never called back after the receptionists put me into voice mails. In another four of them, the receptionists connected me to the wrong people multiple times or flat out told me they didn't know who would be the right person and then didn't offer alternatives. The eighth company is the one we signed the deal with. It was a sixteen-million-dollar-per-year deal, which is now worth closer to forty million per year.

"I never forgot that. Imagine how many deals those companies lost every day because they didn't appreciate the importance of a Director of First Impressions."

Maggie turned to Thomas. "Wasn't Josephine the one who came up with 'Are you talking with a stranger?'"

"She is."

"Josephine came up with that?" I asked. "I always gave you the credit, Thomas. I remember the first time I saw it, I thought it was ingenious. As a matter of fact, the first time I saw it was the same day we were just discussing."

Thomas put down his glass of juice. "That one is all Josephine. She came to me one day and said she had just gotten off the phone with one of our largest customers, and they had remarked that each time they called they felt like they were talking with a friend. I'd been trying to come up with a good way to illustrate the types of relationships I wanted us to have with everyone we interacted with, and she suggested having little signs made up that said 'Are you talking with a stranger?' That way when people were on the phone, it would be a great reminder to make the extra effort to get to know the person on the other end of the call a little better.

"I knew the relationship piece was important. People like doing business with people they like. If we were just another caller from another company, we wouldn't stand out. And if we didn't stand out, we would be too easy to replace. I wanted our customers, our vendors, our fulfillment houses, everybody we interacted with, to not only view us as their friend, but ideally, for our people to actually be their friends in some capacity.

"I wasn't so idealistic I expected to have a one hundred percent success rate, but I also knew if we could get to even a sixty or seventy percent success rate, we would be way ahead of everyone else. The signs were a good step, and they worked great. We still use them. We supplemented those with stipends for lunches so people could invite their counterparts to lunch at the company restaurant and hopefully establish relationships that way. We still do that too."

Thomas smiled. "Sometimes the relationships went a little farther than I think we had envisioned when we came up with the idea. Over the years since we put that in place, there've been more than a few marriages by people whose first face-to-face meeting was a company paid lunch."

"Was that idea the reason you built the restaurants?" I asked.

"No, actually that was a decision we made earlier. I asked the people in the company to come up with some ideas for improving our overall work experience, and building the restaurants was one of their ideas. I was all for it. We won on all kinds of fronts with that one. The restaurants always broke even, the employees got great food that cost them less than if they went outside, so they tended to stay in the building, which meant they were more productive. The food was always healthy, which although I never had any analysis done, I have to believe in some way has helped keep our health-care costs down. And, it gave us a classy place to entertain clients and customers. Maggie actually designed the restaurants, did you know that?"

"I didn't know that. Thomas was a client of your firm, Maggie?"

"He was," she said. "I believe his instructions were something along the lines of 'it needs to meet these needs,' and he handed me a list of requirements his people had come up with. Actually, it was a really fun project. There were so many people working in the company we knew it would be a success if we just designed it the way the people wanted. The average little restaurant only serves about a hundred customers or less over a lunch, and even back then there were almost a thousand people working with Thomas."

"What were the requirements?"

She thought for a moment. "I don't remember all of them, but they were what you might expect. The price of lunch had to be less than the local restaurants, they wanted different ethnic foods, the atmosphere had to be classy, and it had to be at least as fast as eating out."

"Well, you definitely pulled it off. I remember when I met Thomas there for lunch. I was amazed that the restaurants were run by the company. They looked like four nice little independent restaurants." I turned to Thomas. "Weren't you concerned about the cost?"

"No, we had a couple of people on the team who had momentary cases of Leftsideitis, but they got over those pretty quickly once we ran the numbers."

I smiled. "Ah, yes, Leftsideitis. That day at your company was the first time I heard that term too. There were a lot of firsts that day."

"I remember that," Thomas replied. "You bumped into Tim Bankins and you couldn't believe I bought all those books for him."

Maggie turned to me. "I guess I don't know this story either. Who is Tim Bankins?"

"Now he's the president of Pressco, Thomas's publishing company," I said. "Back then he was a guy with a wall of books in his office. After my little saga with Josephine, she gave me a badge which said 'I'm a visitor, hide all the good stuff.' Then, per Thomas's instructions, she told me to wander the halls for thirty minutes and meet as many people as I could. I didn't realize until I started walking around that a visitor's badge got you instant attention in Thomas's companies. Every time someone saw it, they would introduce themselves and ask me if I needed anything. I felt like a rock star.

"Tim was one of the people I met. I happened to walk by his office as he was walking out, and when he introduced himself, I asked why he had so many books in his office. He must have had a hundred of them in there. He explained that fifteen or so dealt with an idea he was working on—which ended up being Pressco. The other ones were all gifts from Thomas. I couldn't believe it. I was even more shocked when he told me Thomas bought everyone in the company at least a book per quarter and sometimes a few extra ones during the year if he came across one he particularly liked.

"So when I eventually met Thomas for lunch in one of the restaurants, I asked him about it and that was the first time I heard about Leftsideitis."

Thomas smiled. "And do you remember what I told you?"

"Thomas, I remember all of our conversations. You explained that most decisions in life are composed of basic math. Is $C + E < O$? C is cost, E is effort, and O is output. Most people get hung up on the C and E and never look at the O. Since C and E are on the left side of the equation, they are suffering from Leftsideitis."

"Very impressive, Joe. I'm glad my words held so much weight with you."

"They did, and also I've now taught that at Fulfill U about ten times."

Maggie looked at Thomas. "What does that have to do with the books?"

"Joe couldn't understand how I could afford to buy more than fifty-six thousand books each year for the people who worked with me. So I had to explain to him if you want to be a CEO, you have to be able to figure out if $C + E < O$. Most people make decisions on how much something costs—the C. Or they get hung up on the effort required to do something—the E. My point to him was, I didn't care how much something costs, or how much effort is required to do it, just so long as the output, the O, is greater than the combination of the cost and the effort. All things taken into consideration, as long as the output is greater, then it's worth doing.

"Since we buy those books in bulk, we get them at major discounts from the publishers. At our price of ten dollars per book, the total expense for the year is almost half a million dollars. At first glance, that might seem like a lot. Half a million dollars is half a million dollars. But when you look at the output, it's a no-brainer investment. I pick good books that have immediate, practical benefit for the people who work with me. So the real question is . . . after reading the four books I buy them, will my people make forty-one dollars or more worth of better decisions, or be forty-one dollars or more productive, or come up with an idea worth forty-one dollars or more regarding how they lead their teams, or be able to solve problems forty-one dollars faster because they now have common references and methods to work with?

"And the answer is, of course they will. I wouldn't buy them books that didn't have at least two hundred dollars' worth of immediate value. So the O far exceeds the C + E and therefore it's a good investment. Plus, they don't just use the information for one year. I make the investment once, but I get the benefit from their improvements for as long as they work with me."

"That was certainly one of the 'Aha!' moments of that day for me," I said. "You cleared up the book question, but it was more the broader implication of the equation that really struck me. I still catch myself sometimes getting caught up in the cost and effort of something and not looking at the output."

I smiled and then paused for dramatic effect. . . . "And then I always hear your voice in my head, Thomas: 'If you want to be a CEO, you have to be able to figure out if C + E < O.' "

Thomas laughed. "Does the voice sound like mine, or is it more angelic, like a guardian angel's voice?"

"More like a mosquito actually. Just right there, buzzing . . . where you can't seem to get rid of it."

Maggie started laughing and rolled her eyes as she shook her head back and forth in mock disappointment. "The two of you. If it's not one, it's the other."

And for just a few minutes, we all forgot why we were together this time.

Chapter Eighteen

LATER THAT AFTERNOON I WAS SITTING ON THE patio reading. Thomas had gone to try to get some sleep.

"Thanks for being here, Joe," Maggie said as she pulled out a chair and joined me at the small table.

"Of course, Maggie. I just wish there was something I could do. I feel a little helpless."

"Just the fact you're here means a lot to us, Joe. This is a strange time, a strange situation."

We sat in silence for a while, watching the birds jump from branch to branch in the large oak tree closest to the house.

She turned and looked at me. "You probably can't see it, but despite all his efforts, Thomas's energy is fading fast, Joe. He tries to cover it, even from me, but I see how much pain he's in, and how he fights to keep his energy up. When you walked into his hospital room the other day, you raised his energy. The way the two of you kid each other and goof around . . ." She smiled. "When he heard your voice that day, his face lit up more than I've seen it in the last month, Joe. You don't need to do anything else. Just by being around you remind him he's so much more than this illness. You help him be him."

I looked at her. She was tired, I could tell. It wasn't just Thomas who was fighting to keep the energy up.

We both watched the birds some more.

"You know, Joe, for some reason that perhaps even the two of you will never figure out, there is a bond between you and Thomas. I think in some ways he sees you like the son he wishes we could have had. In other ways, he sees you like his best friend. And at times I think he sees in you a younger version of himself."

I nodded and smiled. "I remember when I told him I'd decided to take a long break and head off for a few months on my first international backpacking trip. I never thought someone would be so enthused because I was leaving."

Maggie laughed. "I remember that. He told me all about it. How he knew it was a big decision for you and that if you went, he knew you'd get your first true taste of that life you'd been dreaming about for so long."

She smiled. "He also knew he could only take you so far on that journey. You had to be the one to decide for yourself it was what you truly wanted."

I nodded my head. We sat in silence again.

"Maggie, what's going to happen to Thomas?"

She sat silently, and when I looked over, she was crying.

"I'm sorry, Maggie. We don't have to talk about it."

"No, Joe, it is what it is, and pretending it's something else won't help." She wiped the tears from her cheek. "The doctors have told us he will keep getting worse over time. At a minimum it will be gradual. He'll have a harder time maintaining his balance; his vision may be affected as the tumor pushes on his brain. It's likely he'll start to have seizures. They told us we should expect his body will suddenly shut down at times."

Maggie paused and took a long breath. Tears again rolled down her cheeks. "It's not an exact science with this, Joe. But they think he has about four weeks at the most."

Chapter Nineteen

I WALKED INTO THOMAS'S OFFICE AND SAT down at his desk. It had been a few days since my discussion with Maggie, and almost a week since I'd arrived. Thomas had offered up his office as a place for me to catch up on things, and I needed to take care of a few e-mails and phone calls.

As I leaned back in the chair and looked around the room, my eyes stopped at a stack of turquoise blue Post-it notes sitting on the desk. They were the larger ones, about eight inches long and four inches wide.

On the top of the notes, in dark lettering, it said, "From the Desk of Thomas Derale—Your fellow traveler on this amazing journey." I smiled and picked a pack up. A unique part of Thomas's leadership culture revolved around the Thomas Derale Post-it notes.

It had all started with a single person and a single Post-it. Thomas originally had the notes made for his own use. He liked to jot down his comments and ideas and then stick them directly on the particular document he was reading. One day though, just to be funny, he had copied a Dilbert cartoon onto the Post-it and left it on the computer screen of one of his people, along with a scribbled note that said, "Thank you for keeping us from getting to this point."

The woman who received the note was a junior leader who had come up with a unique and effective way of dealing with an IT problem that had been troubling the company. Her response to the note was so gracious Thomas left a few notes for other people. Some were funny things, others were thank-you messages for something the recipient had done. They were just another way for Thomas to connect with his people.

Over time, the notes became a big part of the culture in Thomas's companies. People kept them and posted them in their work area. They prized them in a way. The notes became sort of an inside joke known by people in the company, and they were brought up often by speakers at company events.

As Thomas said, the notes sort of took on a life of their own, and because of that, he carried a pack of them with him wherever he went in his companies.

I smiled and put down the pack of Post-its, then plugged in my laptop. As it loaded up, I scanned the business periodicals on Thomas's desk. The large stack included copies of *The Wall Street Journal*, *Business Week*, *Forbes*, *Executive Excellence* . . . Each had one of his Post-it notes sticking out from the side.

I assumed they were interesting articles Thomas had marked. I picked up the magazine on the top of the stack and flipped to the page with the Post-it note. The title of the article was "How to Boost Profits in 4 Simple Steps." It was coauthored by Thomas and the editor of the magazine.

I started to read.

One of the most common mistakes companies make when they are trying to boost their profits is to try to get new customers. Typically this behavior is a reflection of their history. When they were new, they probably had zero or just a few customers. To survive, they had to get more. Getting new customers made sense.

For companies that are out of survival mode and are instead trying to boost their profitability, acquiring new customers is not the best strategy. Studies by Capgemini and Gartner Group have shown that depending on the industry, it costs three to seven times more money to acquire a new customer than to get an existing customer to make a new purchase.

The best profit-boosting opportunities lie in optimizing the relationships you have with your existing customers. Here are four simple steps to do just that.

STEP #1: FIND AND STRENGTHEN YOUR PILLARS

Do you know which five of your customers contribute the most to your bottom line each year? Can you name them off the top of your head? Can all the employees in your company name them? If not, that is a problem to be addressed, and addressed quickly.

Depending on the size of the organization, a loss of any of the top five customers can range from serious to catastrophic. These clients are the pillars supporting your company. Think of your business as a structure sitting in the middle of shark-infested waters. Five pillars are arranged in a circle and your business balances on top of them. What happens if one or two of those pillars shrink? What happens if one of them goes away completely?

Part of the key to optimizing profits is securing your pillars. If you look at the amount of time your organization spends on customer service and break it down by customer, would you find your pillars are the five customers who get the most service?

Most likely they do not. "Problem customers" usually command the most attention, followed closely by efforts to get new customers. Change that. Allocate your customer service time and attention based on how critical each customer is to your business. Take the resources being applied to the problem customers and focus them on the pillars. Task those people with making your relationships with the pillars so strong they will never crumble. Challenge them to find ways to help the pillars be successful. Be a pillar to your pillars.

STEP #2: INVENTORY YOUR OFFERINGS

Take an inventory of all the products and services you currently provide. Rank them in order of profitability. When all the offerings have been identified, categorize them from one to five. Ones should be the 20 percent of the offerings that are most profitable. Twos will be the next 20 percent, on down to five, which will be those products and services in the bottom 20 percent in terms of profitability.

Now comes the interesting part. Create a grid with clients across the top and offerings down the left side. Arrange the clients in order of how much they impact your bottom line. The most impactful client should be the first one, and the least impactful client should be the last. For the offerings, which are on the left side of the grid, keep them in order of most profitable to least profitable.

When you have finished creating the grid, go through it and for each client, put check marks on the products and services you provide for them. This is your profitability map.

Arrange customers in order of
profitablitiy, starting with your
most profitable on the far left.

5 Pillars

Arrange products and services
in order of profitablity, with the
most profitable ones at the top.

	Customer #1	Customer #2	Customer #3	Customer #4	Customer #5	Customer #6	Customer #7	Customer #N
Product/Service #1								
Product/Service #2								
Product/Service #3								
Product/Service #4								
Product/Service #5								
Product/Service #6								
Product/Service #7								
Product/Service #N								

STEP #3: ATTACK THE GAPS

*Look at your pillars. How are you doing in terms of providing your full
suite of offerings to them? Any boxes without checks represent an opportunity for you to solidify your relationship. Start with the offerings ranked
one and not being used by your pillars, and focus on getting those blanks
filled in.*

*Now look at the rest of your map. Where are the check marks? Where
are the gaps? Every gap represents an opportunity to boost your profits.
Start with the more profitable clients, and try to fill in all the products
and services that are ones and twos. Educate those customers about these
other ways you can serve them. Find out what needs they have and identify ways you can fill them. These efforts will not only strengthen your
relationship, but will also make them more profitable clients for you.*

STEP #4: LEARN FROM YOUR "LOVERS"

As you are implementing step three, take another look at your graph. Find the five customers who use the greatest percentage of your products and services. These are the customers who just love what you do. They represent a tremendous learning opportunity.

There is some reason, or group of reasons, why these customers love you so much. If you can find out those reasons, you can apply that knowledge to the way you interact with the rest of your customers. Perhaps a particular salesperson has figured out something that is really working. Maybe the account representative or customer service contact is particularly good. Whatever the reason is, you need to know.

Interview your "lovers" and learn from them. If they tell you the difference is a particular person in your company, interview that person and find out what he or she does that is working so well.

Within those interviews lies profit-boosting information. Gather it and then apply the learnings to the way you interact with your other customers. The goal is to create more lovers, starting with your pillars, and then working your way across your customer list.

Most organizations acquire customers by filling a single particular need. The key to boosting profits is not to go out and get more of those customers. Find and strengthen your pillars so your organization is well supported, inventory your offerings, fill the gaps, and learn from your lovers. Because those four steps are the way to boost your profits.

Chapter Twenty

I GRABBED ANOTHER MAGAZINE. THIS TIME the Post-it marked an article by Thomas called "Don't Recruit the Best People and Customers—Attract Them."

Smart leaders don't recruit the best people and customers, they attract them. Why do they do it? Because it makes their lives easier, and their companies more successful. How do they do it? They have a clearly defined corporate Purpose For Existing (PFE), they tell the world about it, they live it, and the best people and customers come to them. They don't recruit, they attract.

The success of this method is based on two principles. The first is a basic tenet of life on the planet: "Like attracts like." It is the reason zebras run together on the African plains, similar-looking fish travel in schools, and in any given crowd of people, each subgroup is composed of individuals with similar characteristics. A leader who has defined his or her company's Purpose For Existing or PFE, is saying in essence, "I am a zebra and this is what I'm all about. If you too are a zebra, come out here on the plains and join me."

* * *

I READ the entire article, and as I finished the last line, Thomas walked into the office.

"Don't beat me, I swear I didn't take anything," I joked.

"What, this?" He lifted the cane he was holding. "This just makes me look dapper and stylish for Maggie."

Two days earlier, Thomas had taken a tough fall. It was what Maggie had told me about. The tumor was starting to cause Thomas to have sudden spells where his equilibrium was all off. After the fall, he started keeping the cane with him so he could maintain his balance.

We both knew it. We both didn't want to dwell on it.

I nodded toward the magazines I'd opened. "These are good articles, Thomas."

"Thanks. I thought they turned out well."

"I'm a little surprised you went into as much detail as you did."

"Why is that?"

"Well, the way you do things and what you've taught the people in your companies are part of what has made the companies so successful. Were you worried about giving away a little too much information?"

Thomas sat down in the chair opposite from me. "I talked it over with the CEOs of my companies. As you know, we've always been very open at the executive retreats regarding what's working for us and what isn't. The majority of those attendees are from outside of our organizations. The CEOs and I decided that sharing some of the information through the magazines would be a good way to reach more people.

"My thought was this, Joe. I've learned a lot from other people because they were willing to share what they knew. At the end of the day, it comes down to execution and knowledge. If someone is out there doing a great job of leading, and willing to do what it takes to create a great company, but they just don't know how to optimize their income streams, I'd rather they learn about the five pillars and apply the matrix and get on track, than struggle along and maybe eventually go out of business. There are plenty of opportunities, and there is plenty of money to be made by everyone."

Thomas sighed. "I don't know, Joe. Maybe a year ago when I wrote these articles I already sensed what was happening to me. When you're in this situation, you want to make sure you are closing all the loops, tying up all the loose ends. Someone did me a big favor one time—a life-changing favor—by sharing with me what they knew. I promised them I'd do the same during my lifetime. Now that things are winding down for me, I want to make sure I fulfill that promise all the way through.

"When I'm gone, what I've learned won't help me anymore, Joe. But if I share it with someone else, as long as they're around, it can still help them. And if they end up sharing it with someone else, who knows, maybe it will live for a long time after I'm gone. I like that idea. It makes my life seem more meaningful somehow."

Chapter Twenty-one

I LEFT THOMAS IN HIS OFFICE AND WANDERED out to the backyard. My travel journal was sitting on the table. Thomas had asked if I was keeping one during my trip to Spain, and I'd given it to him to read. Seeing it there reminded me of a conversation we'd had early on in our friendship. It was during my second visit to his company. I'd shared with him I was considering canceling an upcoming vacation because of something at my job. He had looked at me incredulously.

"You know, Joe, one of the funniest things about life is we believe we're immortal. We think we can put things off because there's always more time and other opportunities. But that's one of life's greatest illusions. In our minds, we believe we're twenty-one, or thirty-four, or whatever mental age we stopped counting at. But this experience doesn't go on forever, Joe. It ends at some point.

"You have to do what you want while you can. Do you know one out of every six twenty-year-olds will die before they reach retirement? And nearly thirty percent of the ones who live will be disabled? People work for forty or fifty years so someday they can retire and climb the Eiffel Tower in France, or explore the Australian outback, or wander through the Tower of London. Then they never make it. And too many of those who do make it can only view the sites from the inside of a tour bus, because they don't have the physical ability to walk on their own anymore.

"Leadership isn't about standing on a stage once a year, or sending a video conference thanking all the people who work for you for doing things you don't even know anything about. That would be like a parent who once a year on their child's birthday tells the child they love them. But all year long they do nothing to demonstrate that love. Great leadership, Joe, is about creating an environment where people succeed. Not just once a year, not just when there's extra money left in the budget, but creating that environment every day.

"Joe, did you know ninety-five percent of people have 'travel the world' as one of their Big Five for Life?"

I shook my head no.

"It's true. We have an in-house travel office just to help people in my companies take the trip of their dreams. Not when they are sixty-five and retired, but now, each year. Sometimes many times per year. And you know what, Joe? When they come back, they're even better employees and better people than they were before they left—which is really saying something.

"And the truth is, we've helped them get more than just the experiences they had on their trip, much more. We've helped them build a room in the museum of their life. A good room, Joe. A room they'll visit with joy the rest of their lives. Because when you take that time and get those experiences, no one can ever take them away. You have them forever. But, Joe, once you let that time go, it's gone forever. You can never get it back. Do you know how much of an extra expense is it for us to run the travel office?"

I shook my head again.

"Nothing."

"Nothing?"

"C + E < O. One of my people came to me with the idea after he had taken a three-month sabbatical. Now we have him and five other people running it. They're all travel junkies. They have MBAs from the top schools in the world and stellar résumés, each of them. They could be running divisions in any of my companies or of any other Fortune 500 company for that matter. Instead, they run this division—the Big Five for Life Travel division. Each of them is on for five months and off for seven. They overlap by a month. And they get full health benefits for the whole year. When they aren't here, they're off traveling the world, which is what they love. When they come back, they're busy helping our people go travel around the world, which is something else they love.

"They figured out how to make the whole department self-sufficient through the travel rebates they get from the airline, hotel, and car rental companies. This is part of the environment of success I want for my people, Joe. Not just because it's a good business decision, although it is. Not just because it motivates people and when they're motivated, they're more productive. I want it because in addition to all of that, the truth is as a leader, I'm not just in the business of business. Every leader, no matter what their role, is also in the business of life.

"We can forget about that for a while. Cancel a trip here and there, put off our friends and loved ones now and again . . . But why? I did an interview one time and the interviewer asked me if I had a solution for employee burnout. He couldn't believe it when I told him we didn't have burnout. I shared with him that burnout is caused when people put in long nights working towards something they don't really care about. Something that has only one real benefit to the people working on it: it helps put enough money in their bank account so they can then *stop* doing it.

"Everything in my companies is tied to people's Purpose For Existing and Big Five for Life, Joe. We do things because in the process of doing them we are guaranteeing our life is a success as we define success. I don't want people working with me who *like* their job. I want people whose work *fulfills* them. When you have that, people don't get burned out each day. They get energized.

"Energized people are productive. Burned-out people quit. Which one of those do you think helps you achieve success as a leader?" Thomas gestured to an office across from us. "Do you see that man over there, the one in the blue polo shirt and the gray pants?"

I looked toward the office. "Yes, I see him."

"That's Chris Lanticks." Thomas walked to a side hallway. "Look over here."

I moved to where Thomas was pointing. The entire hallway was covered with pictures. It looked as if all the people were on vacation.

"This is our Big Five for Life travel wall. Everyone who wants to can put up pictures of where they went. The idea is to inspire others to fulfill their travel dreams." Thomas pointed to a picture of Chris. "Here's Chris and his wife in Australia. They went for six weeks last year."

"He gets six weeks of vacation?"

"No, he gets four weeks. He decided to take his laptop with him, dial in a few times for conference calls, and extend his trip for an extra two weeks that way."

"Who kept track of him?"

Thomas laughed. "He kept track of himself. Talented people don't need someone monitoring their behavior, Joe. They don't do a great job because someone's watching them. They do a great job because that's who they are, and they like what they do."

Chapter Twenty-two

IT WAS NOW THREE WEEKS SINCE I'D STARTED staying with Maggie and Thomas. During that time I'd seen Thomas handle some company-related issues by phone, but he hadn't gone into his corporate office. Maggie told me it was a combination of things. Thomas didn't want his people to watch him decline, and he was also in a lot of pain most of the time. So I was surprised one afternoon when he asked if I was free the next night to attend a meeting.

"Sure, Thomas, what's going on?"

"Cindy Ronker has scheduled a Make Me Better meeting for a new idea she's working on. She wanted to know if I would attend. I told her you were in town and she asked me to see if you would participate as well."

"Love to. MMBs are always a lot of fun." I looked at Thomas. I hesitated to ask him, but I did anyway. "Are you sure you're up to it? The last few days seemed like they were pretty tough on you."

Maggie had shared with me Thomas wasn't sleeping much. He tried to, but the pain was often intolerable. And with his equilibrium being thrown out of balance, when he would lie down to try to sleep, he would often feel as if he were falling, or the room were spinning. His body was shutting down.

"I'll be fine, Joe. The doctors have sent over something different for the pain. They say I can't use it nonstop, but if I take it, the impact will last for two to three hours." Thomas smiled wearily. "I need to get out, Joe. The past three days aren't how I want to end this journey. I want to go do something. I invented the Make Me Better. This is the last one I'll see, and I don't want to miss it."

With that statement, Thomas crossed a new threshold. Up until then we both knew he was dying. Yet I think—as he had shared with me that day in his office when he'd told me we all believe we are immortal—some small part of him had still believed something might change. He believed there was still a chance. Over the last few days he had decided this was truly it.

My phone rang and I looked at the caller ID. It was Sonia. She and I had spoken twice since our conversation on the flight. Both times she'd called to see how Thomas was doing. Even though she'd only heard about him and seen him on the video, she was genuinely concerned about him. Thomas had that effect on people.

"Thomas, do you remember the woman I mentioned from the plane? Sonia? I think she'd get a lot out of seeing something like the MMB. And I know she'd like to meet you. Are you up for the idea of her going with us?"

Thomas chuckled. "Joe, you know once I'm gone you're going to have to get your own dates."

I smiled and shook my head back and forth. "I'll take that as a yes."

Chapter Twenty-three

THE NEXT NIGHT, THOMAS ARRANGED FOR A CAR service to pick us up. Twenty minutes later we were in front of Sonia's place.

"Hello, Thomas," she said as she entered the car and slid onto the black leather seat of the limousine. "I'm Sonia. It's a pleasure to meet you." I slid in behind her and the driver shut the door.

Thomas took her extended hand into both of his. "It's a pleasure to meet you as well, Sonia. I'm glad you could join us."

She looked at me and then at Thomas. "You're sure I won't be intruding?"

"Not at all," Thomas replied. "Although I hope Joe shared with you that everyone who is invited to a Make Me Better session can't just attend. They have to participate."

Sonia looked at me. "No . . . actually he left that part out. He didn't tell me much actually, other than he thought I'd find it interesting. What exactly am I in for?"

Thomas looked at me. "Why don't you explain it, Joe? I'll jump in at random intervals." A moment before, while Sonia was speaking, I'd seen him cringe from an unexpected bout of pain. I'd looked at him and opened my mouth to ask if he was okay, but he'd just moved his head back and forth slightly and motioned toward Sonia.

"Alright," I said, trying to sound energetic. "I'll do the honors. What you are about to participate in is a Thomas Derale original. He came up with the concept for the Make Me Better, or MMB as you'll probably hear it called, back when he had his first company. It's been part of the culture ever since. As I explained on the phone, each of Thomas's fourteen companies has evolved out of an idea from someone in one of his existing companies. All of them have gone through a MMB. Tonight you're going to see what may become the fifteenth company."

"You're going to help create what may become the fifteenth company," Thomas corrected me. "No attendees, remember. Just participants."

Sonia looked at Thomas and then at me. "So what is this MMB I'll be participating in?"

Thomas nodded in my direction and I continued, "Do you remember the Big Five for Life story I shared with you on the plane, Sonia?"

She nodded. "I do."

"This is an extension of that. One of the principles associated with the Big Five for Life is when you know where you are in life, and you know where you want to go—your Big Five for Life—there is a very important question you need to ask."

"How do I get there?" Sonia interjected.

"Another victim," Thomas said, and smiled.

"Another victim?" Sonia replied.

I jumped in. "Yes, Sonia, I'm afraid you just became a victim of *Mad How* disease."

Sonia started to laugh. "Mad How disease?"

"That's right, Mad How disease. One of the keys to fulfilling your Big Five for Life is to get from where you are, to where you want to go. Most people start by asking the same question you did—'How do I get there?' The problem with asking that question is you end up facing all kinds of unknown obstacles and learning curves. Think of them as mountains. As you face the first couple of them, your enthusiasm and energy are really high, so you struggle up the learning curves and climb over the unknown obstacles. But Sonia, what happens to most people around the third mountain?"

"They get tired of climbing."

"And then what?"

"They give up."

"Exactly," I replied. "And then that great idea for a new company, or exciting adventure, never materializes. It never becomes a reality. Yet another victim of Mad How disease."

Sonia smiled. "So how does one avoid this dreaded Mad How disease?"

"By finding your Who's," I replied. "You find someone who has done, seen, or experienced what you want to do, see, or experience, or something close to it, and you ask them what they did. Then you use that information to fly over the obstacles and race up the learning curves."

"And this works?"

"You'll see it in action tonight," Thomas said with a smile.

Chapter Twenty-four

AS THE DRIVER SLOWED IN FRONT OF THE LARGE building before us, Sonia looked out at it. "Is this your company headquarters, Thomas?"

"No," he replied. "This is one of my other companies. We usually hold the MMBs at the headquarters. I'm not sure why they decided to have it here tonight."

When the car stopped, Sonia and I climbed out. Thomas followed slowly. He had his cane with him. "Do I look stylish?" he asked me, and lifted the cane slightly.

"Incredibly," I replied. "It's a good thing Maggie isn't here. We'd have to get the two of you a hotel room."

The receptionist at the entrance greeted us with a smile. "Hello, Thomas," she said warmly, and came out from behind the desk and gave him a hug. "I stuck around just so I could see you tonight."

"Hello, Emily," Thomas replied. He introduced Sonia and Emily. "Emily has been here since the first day this company was formed, almost ten years ago. She keeps the place together."

Emily smiled and took Thomas's arm. "Since you're still playing this whole sympathy angle, let me walk you to the MMB meeting.

Honestly, Thomas, I think people are going to see through this illness thing."

"I don't know," he replied. "I think I can pull this off for a while."

Sonia and I walked behind them as Emily and Thomas bantered back and forth.

"Is it like that with Thomas and all his people?" Sonia asked, surprised.

"Pretty much," I replied. "Thomas has a philosophy that the world would be a better place if everyone knew each other on a first-name basis."

"It's not just that," Sonia said. "He's the head of all of these companies and she's the receptionist. The way they tease each other, you'd think he and Emily were neighbors, or old friends."

"That's Thomas. If you asked him, he'd say they *are* old friends. She's shared ten years of her life with this company."

"She gets paid, doesn't she?"

"Of course."

"So . . ."

"Sonia, I know it may seem radical. It seemed radical to me when I first met Thomas and saw what it was like when you walk through one of his companies. He designed his life so the better his companies do, the more his own personal Purpose For Existing is fulfilled. So from his perspective, each person who shows up each day and works with him is helping him fulfill his PFE. Sure they get paid. Sure they are fulfilling their own Purpose For Existing and Big Five for Life by being here, or they couldn't have gotten the job. But Thomas never forgets they always have a choice, and they choose to be here. So he always makes them feel welcome and always thanks them for helping him fulfill his Purpose For Existing."

Sonia looked up ahead at Emily. "You don't by any chance know her Big Five for Life, do you?"

"Actually, she has a pretty amazing story. I don't remember all the details, but ten years ago she sent Thomas a letter. She wrote she'd learned about him from an interview she'd read in the *Chicago Tribune*. In the letter she explained she was a single mom, and her daughter and son-in-law had been killed in a car accident. The story of the accident was in the paper the same day as the interview with Thomas.

"Her daughter's little eight-year-old girl survived the accident and was now her responsibility. She shared she had a terrible boss and a terrible job, and she didn't know what to do. She wrote out her Big Five for Life, which included making people happy, finding a way for her granddaughter to go to college, and finding a way for her to keep her granddaughter safe every day. She shared the other two also, but I don't remember what they were."

"And he hired her?"

"No, he called her personally and invited her to lunch at the company restaurant. Then he sent a car and driver to pick her up. When they met for lunch, he went over her PFE and Big Five for Life with her. And by the time they were done, he told her he thought she would make a great Director of First Impressions at the new company being formed. He told her he couldn't promise her the job, because it was up to Kerry Dobsin, the new CEO of that company. But he would set up a meeting, which he did."

"And then she got hired."

"She did. And then Thomas and Kerry got together with Emily and started an on-site after-school club where kids of parents who worked in Thomas's companies could hang out and do their homework after school. So she got to make people happy every day by being the positive first impression people would have of the new company. Her salary provided her with a means of paying for her granddaughter to go to college. And the on-site club she helped start, gave her granddaughter a safe place to stay when she was done with school."

Sonia nodded. "Is Kerry still the head of this company?"

"No, actually now she's the COO for the overarching organization that connects all the companies. She'll probably be here tonight. I'll introduce you."

Sonia paused and looked at me. "Joe, I don't want to sound cynical . . . but . . . all of the things Thomas and Kerry did for Emily. Was that really the best use of their time? He's the owner of how many companies? And she was the CEO of one of the companies."

"That's Thomas," I answered. "And because that's Thomas and that's the culture he has created, that's Kerry too. Trust me, Emily is one amazing Director of First Impressions, and I'm sure you could calculate how much that has meant financially in terms of new clients, and therefore justify why it was worth Thomas's time. You could probably do the same for the on-site after-school club they created. I'm sure having it gives parents a lot of peace of mind and decreases absenteeism, which both translate into higher productivity and therefore more profits.

"I think more likely, though, if you asked Thomas and Kerry about it, they'd tell you successful leaders are the ones who get out of the mind-set they're just in the business of business and realize they're also in the business of life. And because of that, the financial results follow."

Chapter Twenty-five

SONIA AND I CAUGHT UP WITH THOMAS AND Emily as they were approaching the door to the conference room.

"Sounds like a party in there," Sonia said.

It did sound like a party. Music was playing and people were laughing and talking.

"MMBs are always a party," I said, and smiled.

I opened the door to the room and a chorus of yells erupted. As Thomas walked in, he was instantly greeted by the men and women in the room. They were smiling and laughing as they came up and hugged him, shook his hand, joked with him.

I turned to Sonia. "This is what I meant by more than just the business of business. These people aren't just employees. They're fellow travelers helping each other travel very similar journeys."

Sonia and I stood by the door where we entered, and I let her take in the scene. We were in a theater-style classroom with two large screens on each side of the front of the room. In front of the screens, chairs were arranged in semicircles on tiered platforms so each row was about a foot and a half higher than the row in front of it.

On the screen to the far right an animated video was playing.

Someone had superimposed Thomas's head on an animated cartoon character dressed in khaki clothing. The character was walking around in the jungle and kept looking behind trees and rocks. Every few seconds a lion or elephant or some other animal would appear. On the top of the screen it said, "Thomas in the pursuit of his Big Five for Life."

Sonia tapped my shoulder and pointed to it. "What's that about?" she asked with a smile.

I laughed. "The original idea for the Big Five for Life comes from that book I told you about. The one with the young man and Ma Ma Gombe. The whole story takes place in Africa."

Sonia laughed out loud. "And that one?" She pointed to the other screen.

On the other screen was the heading "Where in the world is Joe Pogrete?" An equally enterprising IT person had superimposed a picture of my face onto a cartoon character who was wandering across a giant map of the world. Every few seconds the cartoon character would jump up and down, throw out its arms and legs, and my voice would come on saying, "This is Joe Pogrete and I'll be out of the office. . . . This is Joe Pogrete and I'll be out of the office. . . ."

"Sorry, Joe, we just couldn't resist once we heard you had returned to us from one of your four-month sabbaticals," a voice said.

I turned to see Kerry Dobsin, the COO I had mentioned to Sonia. She hugged Thomas and then came over and hugged me hello.

"I take it that's right off of my voice-mail message?" I asked laughingly.

Kerry laughed too. "Directly. You made it easy for us."

I introduced Kerry and Sonia. After a few minutes of conversation, Kerry turned to me. "Joe, why don't you let Thomas and me introduce Sonia around while you're getting set up."

"Set up?" I asked.

"Sure. I was going to lead this, but now that you're here . . ."

I smiled. "Excellent. What, I get a whole fifteen minutes to prep for this?"

Kerry smiled back. "Come on, Joe, that's why you get the big bucks." She turned to Sonia. "We usually have these around the time of the executive retreats. Joe has led almost every MMB for the last four years. Fifteen minutes is probably ten minutes more than he needs to get ready. You're in for a treat."

As Kerry walked with Sonia and introduced her to the twenty or so other people, I glanced around the room. Thomas was standing with his weight on his cane while talking with a small crowd of people. He looked okay. A little tired, but okay. I spotted the sponsor for the MMB and went to talk with her. After a few minutes in which she gave me some background information on what she was proposing, I found the microphone and tapped it a few times. "Please take your seats. This is not a drill. I repeat. This is not a drill." Some people in the room laughed, and they all filtered down to the front rows and found places to sit.

The room quieted down. "Good evening, everybody," I began. "Welcome to tonight's MMB. I know most of you are intimately familiar with how this works, because you've had your own MMB and attended many others. For the sake of the few folks who are here for the first time, let me just quickly explain how this works. Every six months, or sooner if one is needed, the CEOs from all of Thomas's companies get together with the specific goal of helping a colleague make a new idea better. Hence the MMB—Make Me Better. The idea can be for a new product, a new service, an operational improvement—really anything that on the surface appears to have some significant potential. As all of you CEOs know, because you all went through this with your ideas, it can also be an idea for starting a new company.

"The format is simple. The person presenting the idea has twenty minutes to explain it. Then the objective of the group is to make it better. Identify opportunities that might not have been mentioned, such as markets that would be a good fit, ways to enhance the idea if it is a product or service offering, possible flaws you see, ways in which your company or your company's customers could benefit from this idea. Remember, the idea is we all have blinders. But we all have different blinders. What might be an obstacle for one person is an opportunity for someone else.

"Also, keep in mind the goal is to make it better, not shoot it down. So if you see a flaw, explain it, and provide some possible alternatives. No negativity. Once this is over, if there are still possible flaws, the presenter can go back and check them out."

I introduced the presenter. He was a twenty-eight-year-old director. He had presented the idea to Cindy Ronker, the CEO of the company where he worked. She liked it and so she brought him here. Over the next twenty minutes he explained his idea. He had prepared well; his presentation was thought out, his analysis was thorough, and he was honest about what he knew and what he needed help on. I watched as he was presenting. Almost everyone in the room was taking notes and writing down ideas, including Sonia.

"Excellent," I said when he had finished and the applause had died down. "Great idea, great presentation." I turned to the audience. "Let's help him make it better. Who has something?"

Instantly, hands went up all over the room. I pointed to one. "Chris."

"You could expand the market to include women under the age of thirty if you . . ."

Another hand went up.

"Stephanie."

"If you go after the market you mentioned, we could joint-market with you. We have over forty thousand names and addresses of people from the promotional campaign we did where . . ."

Another hand.

"Mike."

"The market penetration number might be too high. We did something similar and it ended up being four percent. What you could try is . . ."

For two and a half hours the people in the room worked together to enhance the original idea. After just an hour, they were already enhancing their own enhancements. By the time they were done, six flaws had been identified and fixed, four major enhancements had been made, and eight of the CEOs had identified opportunities to leverage their existing customer base to bring the idea to fruition.

To an outsider, the entire event would have seemed more like a party than a meeting. It was fun, people laughed, they kidded each other. They also worked together perfectly. And in two and a half hours they moved the idea further along than the young man could have done in probably a year on his own.

Chapter Twenty-six

WHEN THE MMB WAS FINISHED AND PEOPLE HAD said their good-byes, Sonia, Thomas, and I climbed into the limousine. Sonia turned to Thomas. "That was amazing. I mean really amazing. I've never seen anything like that."

Thomas smiled. "Thank you, Sonia. I'm glad you enjoyed yourself. And I'm glad you participated." He turned to me. "And thank you, Joe. As always, you did a great job of facilitating the process and helping improve the idea."

"You really did, Joe," Sonia added. "It was fun to watch you up there. Certainly a man in his element."

I laughed. "I have Thomas to thank for that. Like I mentioned on the plane, he helped me find what would be the best fit with my PFE and Big Five for Life."

Thomas smiled and faced Sonia. "What you saw tonight is just the first of three MMBs that the young man who presented will go through. Over the next six months he'll go through something similar with a cross section of people from our different companies, and then with a group of clients who are potential users of the idea. After that he'll come back for one final round with the CEOs."

"How do you select the people who participate?" she asked.

"It's a lottery system. We had so many volunteers that now we randomly select twenty for each MMB. Those sessions are done during the day."

Sonia looked at both of us. "I can't believe how the CEOs worked together. You'd never see that where I'm employed."

Thomas shifted his cane. "Leadership rolls downhill, Sonia. I never tolerated having people who didn't work together. It's bad for morale, bad for productivity, and in general just bad for business." He chuckled. "Plus it's not much fun that way. The energy, laughter, and enthusiasm you saw tonight are the same that existed when my first company consisted of me and two other people."

"So is it just cultural?" Sonia asked.

"That's a big part of it, but there's more too," Thomas replied. "Each of those CEOs comes to the MMBs partly because what comes around goes around. Their initial idea for their company went through that exact exercise, and without it they wouldn't have gotten where they are. So they come to these to give back. Plus they get a lot of great ideas to take back to their own companies. And in many cases, as you saw tonight, they get new partnership opportunities."

Sonia looked at Thomas. "So this is how all of your companies were created?"

"It's part of it. Each of those CEOs at some point came up with an original idea that was put through the MMB process. The idea was improved upon and enhanced, and eventually we decided to start a company around it."

She nodded. "Why start other companies? Why not just make them divisions of your original company?"

"A number of reasons. Sometimes it was a branding issue where it made more sense to start a completely different brand. Other times it was a legal reason where we wanted to limit liability. Mostly though, Sonia, I did it that way because I teach my people to be leaders, and at some point great leaders want to lead. They want to give it a shot as not just the head of a division, but as the final decision maker, the CEO.

"Back when it was just my original company, I sensed some of my leaders were within a couple of years of that point. So I gathered them together and we had a two-day, very open and honest, heart-to-heart MMB session on leadership. I told them I didn't want to lose them, but I didn't want to hold them back either. They told me they didn't want to leave because they loved what they had helped build and were a part of. However, they also wanted the opportunity to have ultimate responsibility as a leader."

"So you were right in addressing it," Sonia said.

"Not entirely," Thomas replied. "My thought process was correct, but I had underestimated how close my leaders were to being ready. I thought they were within a couple of years of wanting to lead a full company. Some of them were already there. I almost blew it."

"But you didn't," I said.

Thomas chuckled. "Sometimes you get lucky." He turned to Sonia. "Once that was on the table, we all realized it was in all of our best interests to figure out a solution. So, just like you saw tonight, we started proposing ideas and then we'd make them better. We tweaked and twisted and enhanced them until we came up with something that met our objectives and set us up for success."

"Which was?" Sonia asked.

"A hybrid model," Thomas replied. "Do you remember on the drive here we were talking about avoiding Mad How disease?"

Sonia nodded.

"Well, we did a lot of looking to find some Who's we could imitate. Franchise companies, network marketing, affiliates . . . One of the Who's we imitated is a restaurant chain called Lettuce Entertain You. My wife, Maggie, loves to eat at a place in downtown Chicago called Big Bowl. She used to live near Rush Street and Elm, and there's one right over there. One night we'd talked with our server and she told us the same owners who owned Big Bowl also owned other restaurants. I did a little research and it turned out they had all kinds of different 'restaurant concepts' as they call them.

"I think now they have over thirty of them. Each concept is a unique restaurant with its own décor, style, name, type of food . . . Even its own target market of consumers. And I mean they are completely different. Big Bowl has all kinds of Asian fusion cuisine. They have others that are high-end Italian food and others that specialize in crêpes. All really different, and yet they have a few things in common. The food is always excellent. The service is always great, *and* they all have the same owner.

"What I thought was so ingenious about their concept was even people who love a particular restaurant get tired of eating there. By offering alternative cuisines via alternate restaurants, and offering them in unique ways, they avoided the issue of looking like a chain restaurant, and yet got one of the benefits chains get, which is having multiple locations in a relatively small geographical area."

I turned to Sonia. "They realized people were going to go to other restaurants, so better to cannibalize their own market, than to have their customers going to a competitor. Other companies do this too. Marriott, the huge hotel and resort company does something similar. They will build a Courtyard by Marriott, a Fairfield Inn, and a Residence Inn, all right next to each other. I've seen it where they own three of the four corners at an expressway intersection. They've figured out not all customers are looking for the same type of accommodations, so instead of offering one type and losing customers to their competitors, they are their own competitor. They offer all types and cannibalize their own business to themselves."

Sonia smiled at Thomas. "So how did you apply this to your upcoming leaders?"

"Well, we created a model where leaders who had an idea for a company, including something completely different from my core company, could put it through the four MMB sessions while they were still in their regular job. And if everything looked good, they dedicated four straight Fridays and as much of their own time as they wanted toward the goal of launching the company without requiring any investment capital."

"That's one of the parts I've always found most ingenious," I said.

"That was another Who," Thomas replied. "One of my leaders had heard a speaker named Bruce Hurley explain how he'd started over a dozen companies with no money. Bruce's philosophy is you don't need office space, logos, computers, etc., to start a business. What you need is a good idea, some sweat equity, and a customer. So we adopted that methodology. Every one of my companies was profitable from the very first day. The leaders would use those Fridays to pitch the business idea to potential customers. Often those customers were some of our existing clients who had been identified by leaders in the MMB sessions.

"We already had excellent relationships with those customers, so it was simply a question of did the new product or service fill a need they had? It was the perfect testing ground for a new company.

"If everything looked good after those four Fridays, we'd launch the new company in a section of the corporate headquarters we'd set aside for just that purpose. If three months later everything was still looking good, my initial company made a capital investment in exchange for a percentage of ownership in the new company, and the leader made the decision about where they wanted the company to be headquartered. After that, the company was on its own."

Thomas laughed. "The ones who had it tough were the first few leaders who started their companies. Our last company that launched had the benefit of tapping into customers from thirteen other companies. Those original leaders didn't have as much to tap into. Of course now they get the benefit of tapping into all the new customers the new companies have acquired."

"So the leaders do work together?" Sonia asked.

"They do. That was one of our major goals in that initial meeting. We knew we wanted a system where it was to everyone's benefit to work together. As a matter of fact, the way it's structured now, one and a half percent of each company's annual revenue, including my original company, goes toward finding additional ways for all the companies to benefit from each other. We have a rotational program where each company sends one of their top people to be a member of a team that helps facilitate the process. And, all the CEOs meet every year and run the whole process through a MMB. We enhance it based on what we've learned during the year and iron out any problems that have come up.

"The total benefit looks something like this, Sonia. I trained my people to be leaders. If I hadn't come up with a way for them to take on full leadership responsibilities, some of them would have left eventually. There would be no benefit to me or my company in that situation. With the ones who didn't leave, I'd eventually have a problem where I had a group of great leaders at the top, and therefore no place for my younger leaders to grow into. Then the future leaders would leave and there would be no benefit to me or my company. This way, every time a leader launches a new company, it gives them a chance to lead. It also opens up new spots for my younger leaders. There is a financial benefit to my original company because we own part of each new company, and the better the new company does, the better it is for all my companies, because they all work together."

"You cannibalized your own company," Sonia said.

"In a way, although it wasn't just my decision," Thomas replied. "What I just explained is the result of what came out of the two-day MMB I had with my leaders. They're the ones who designed it. They didn't want to completely separate from what they called 'the family we helped build,' and I didn't want them to be completely separate."

He smiled. "This way they both run their own companies and are still part of 'the family.'"

Thomas leaned back in his seat and reached for one of the bottles of water on the small limousine bar. Suddenly his whole body clenched up and sweat began to pour down his forehead. In just a moment his face had turned white.

"Thomas, what is it?" I asked.

He tried to answer, but couldn't. His eyes rolled back into their sockets.

"Thomas!" I yelled, and grabbed his arm. There was no response. "Thomas!"

I pounded on the sliding-glass partition separating us from the driver.

"Northwestern Memorial Hospital!" I yelled when the driver slid the partition open. "As fast as you can. Northwestern Memorial Hospital!"

Chapter Twenty-seven

SONIA AND I WERE SITTING IN THE WAITING room when Maggie came in. She'd been downtown when I called her from the car and was at the emergency room when we arrived. The doctors had rushed Thomas into the ER for some tests, and Maggie had gone with him. Sonia and I had waited outside. I stood up when she walked in. "Is he alright?" I asked.

She nodded, with tears in her eyes. Sonia stood too and wrapped her arms around Maggie. Maggie burst into tears. "He's dying, Joe. He's as alright as you can be when you're dying."

Sonia guided Maggie to a chair. "Did they say what happened? He seemed perfectly fine. He was talking about his companies, and then all of a sudden . . ."

Maggie wiped the tears from her cheek. "They said it's just the disease progressing. His pain will become worse, the seizures like he had tonight will become more frequent. . . . They told us this would be coming, they just didn't know when."

"What can we do, Maggie?" I asked.

"Nothing." She began to cry again. "That's what makes this so hard. There's nothing any of us can do except be here for him—

help him go out in the way he wants to go out."

She wiped her eyes. "He loved tonight, Joe. I talked with him once the doctors had brought him out of the seizure. He loved seeing the people so full of life, so fulfilled by what they do. He loved watching you up there, Joe. He said he can't imagine a world in which you didn't have the chance to inspire people like you do at the executive retreats, and help them bring forth their ideas like you did tonight. He's so proud of you. He's so proud of all of those people."

I DROPPED Sonia off at her place and then went back to Thomas and Maggie's house. Thomas was staying overnight at the hospital and Maggie was staying with him. It was almost two in the morning and everything was quiet. As I walked around the house, it all seemed pointless. The MMB session, the magazines with Thomas's articles, *The Wall Street Journal* sitting in the living room.

And it struck me that for too many people it all was pointless. But not for Thomas. He had created a life in which everything he did was aligned with his Purpose For Existing—where his activities fulfilled his Big Five for Life. He focused on the people and things that were meaningful to him. Yes, he was dying. But at least while he was alive, he'd truly been living.

"I wonder how many people tonight can say that?" I said out loud.

Chapter Twenty-eight

I WOKE UP LATE THE NEXT MORNING AND WENT for a run. When I returned, I saw Thomas's and Maggie's things by the door. They were back from the hospital.

I walked down the hall, and as I passed Thomas's office, I heard him on the phone. When I glanced in through the open door, he looked up and waved for me to come in. I sat in the chair next to his desk as he finished the call.

"It's true. . . . I appreciate that. . . . Maybe not all three the same day, but we can give it a try. . . . I wouldn't expect you to. . . . Treat it like any other one. . . . Okay, sounds good, see you there."

He hung up the phone and smiled. "Morning, Joe."

"Morning, Thomas, how are you feeling? You scared us a little last night. I figured the doctors would have you sleeping all day today. Instead it looks you're already wheeling and dealing this morning?"

He smiled. "Sort of. The doctors told me to take it easy. I told them there'd be plenty of that soon enough. Any interest in spending a little time at the CBS building tomorrow?"

"Sure, what's going on?"

"That was Mark Whitley from the television show *The Business of Business*. Do you remember him? I did a few different interviews there over the last five or six years."

"I think so. Is he the one that's on in the evenings? Good interviewer, fair guy, asks tough questions?"

"That's him."

"What's going on?"

"He's been asking me for a year to come back and do a segment on leadership in the twenty-first century. Apparently he found out I've been spending a little more time than normal in hospitals, and so he'd like to do the segment sooner than later. Three segments, actually. I don't think I'm up for taping all three at once, but I should be able to do two tomorrow and one the next day. I'd like you to be there if you're up for it."

I nodded. "I'm in."

WE SHOWED up at the studio the next morning at nine thirty. Mark met us in one of the guest waiting rooms.

"Hello, Thomas, good to see you."

Thomas shook his hand. "It's good to see you too, Mark. Thanks for flying all the way out here for this."

"Not a problem. I don't do it often, but under the circumstances . . ." He paused, a little unsure of what to say next.

Thomas saved him. "Mark, that may be the only time I ever see you at a little bit of a loss for words."

Mark smiled. "Well, anyway, we'll tape here and then it will be broadcast nationwide from the studio in New York. We'll edit today's first taping and run it tonight. Then we'll tape one more, which will air tomorrow. We'll just have to see how you feel in terms of when to tape the third one."

Thomas gestured to me. "This is a good buddy of mine, Joe Pogrete. He's a longtime friend and also heads up our executive-seminar division. You should probably be interviewing him and not me."

Mark smiled and he and I shook hands. "Maybe we'll get you in the studio after this airs and talk about what *really* happens in Thomas's companies," he said.

I smiled back. "Happy to, although I'm sure you'll hear plenty of it straight from Thomas."

Mark turned to Thomas. "Speaking of that, like I said on the phone, I know you're not in the best of health at the moment. As a friend I'd like to take it a little easy on you. As a broadcaster, though, there are some tough questions people will be expecting me to ask."

Thomas smiled. "Don't treat me any different now than you would have at any other time, Mark. I'm still the same me."

Mark looked at both of us. "Okay. Well, in that case, let's get you to the studio and get a microphone on you. We'll test for audio and light levels and then we'll start shooting. Joe, feel free to grab a chair next to the cameras once the filming starts."

I watched as Thomas and Mark got situated on the set. It had always amazed me how different things looked in a studio compared to how they appeared on TV. In reality the set was a tiny stage in a giant room of cables, cameras, and monitors, all connected to a control room full of other monitors and audio equipment. On TV it looked like two people sitting in an office having a conversation.

The director counted down the seconds until shooting began. "And cameras kick off in five, four, three, two . . ." On the count that would have been one, he pointed to Mark.

"Good evening, everyone, and welcome to The *Business of Business*. I'm Mark Whitley. Today is the first of our three-part series on

'Leadership in the Twenty-first Century.' My guest for the series is Thomas Derale, CEO and founder of Derale Enterprises. Thomas, good to have you back."

The cameras panned to Thomas and he smiled. "Good to be back, Mark."

"Thomas, people have called your style of leadership a radical departure from the norm. There have even been claims the example you've set is bad for the business world. How do you respond to that?"

So much for easing into the interview, I thought.

Thomas smiled again. "I have to assume that's my competitors who are making those comments, Mark. My people have built fourteen companies that are extremely profitable, our combined turnover rate is nineteen percentage points lower than the industry average, and we have great relationships with the people we do business with. In my mind that's not radical. It means we're doing something right. I'm not sure why anyone would say that's bad for the business world."

Mark turned to the camera. "But what about the 'killer instinct,' and pushing people to perform better? It seems you spend a lot of time on what most people consider the soft skills."

Thomas leaned in toward Mark. "Can I tell you a little secret, Mark?"

I knew what was coming. It was the same thing I had told Sonia on the plane.

"First of all, there's nothing soft about hard profits. Second, all the profits are in the people."

Mark smiled. "Surprising words from a leader so known for the degree to which his people love him. That was a lot of emphasis on profits."

"Mark, think of it this way. If a company isn't profitable, then no matter how great the environment may be, no matter how much the people may love working there, how fulfilling their job may be, pretty soon, the company is going to run out of money, and close. In that scenario everybody loses.

"However, the incorrect belief I see a lot of is that profits and satisfied people are inversely proportional. Too many leaders think the harder you drive people, the more they will do, and therefore the higher the profits will be. They also think the more satisfied people are, the less someone must be driving them, and therefore profits will be less."

"And you don't believe that's true?" Mark replied.

"I know it's not true. If you have to drive people that hard to do their job, then you've either got the wrong people, or you've got the right people doing the wrong job."

Thomas paused. "Mark, do you want me to spill it all? Do you want to hear what the secret formula is for how we've dominated our industries; why so many people think what we do is radical?"

Mark looked a little surprised. I think he thought he was going to have to coax that information out of Thomas.

"Let's hear it."

"For starters, I don't want you to think I've made this any simpler than it really is. What I'm going to tell you is exactly how we do it. This is the philosophy I used to start our parent company, and it's exactly how the other thirteen were formed."

"Okay," Mark said.

"For starters, I figured out what the heck I wanted to do with my life. What would make me happy? Why was I here? What would make me so fulfilled that at the end I would die feeling like I had really lived life to the fullest? Then I figured out which business models would enable me to make the most money while I was doing those things, and I put them in place."

Thomas stopped speaking. Mark looked at him, unsure whether he was done.

"That's it?"

"That's it. That's the secret." Thomas paused. "Now do you want to know why it works?"

Mark smiled. "I think our viewers would like that."

"Is it more enjoyable to do something you like, or don't like, Mark?"

"Something you like."

"When you like to do something, do you want to do it right away, or procrastinate doing it?"

"You want to do it right away."

Thomas smiled. "Me too, Mark. I started a company doing something I liked. I was good at making money doing things I didn't like, so I figured I should be a raging success when I was actually spending my time on something I cared about. And it worked. I was productive, I was efficient, people liked my enthusiasm. . . . It worked so well that when I started to hire people to work with me, I only hired people who liked to do the things I needed done."

Mark jumped in when Thomas finished his sentence. "Alright, Thomas, I can see how having people doing jobs they like would make them more productive, and productivity leads to higher profits, but is it realistic to think you can find people who really love their job? And is it realistic that without some type of discipline they'll really do their job?"

Thomas rotated a bit in his chair. "The answer to your first question is—without a doubt. The answer to your second question is—without a doubt. For everything you hate to do, there is someone out there who loves to do it. Do you hate filing? There are people out there who live to see things organized. It makes their day, it brings them incredible joy. Hire one of them. Do you need to create new product ideas but hate the idea of sitting in brainstorming meetings? Hire someone whose brain is constantly full of ideas but they have no outlet for them.

"Regarding whether or not they'll do the job without someone hounding them—they will if their job fulfills part of their Big Five for Life."

Mark shuffled some of the pieces of paper in front of him and pulled one out. "I'm glad you brought that up, Thomas. You are known for many things, including some of your sayings." He glanced at the paper. "One of which is, 'What are your Big Five for Life?' Let's talk about that one, and then I've got some other ones to ask you about."

Thomas nodded, then explained what the Big Five for Life was and how he had incorporated it into his companies. When he finished, Mark laughed. "That sounds like you're hiring people to do the things they do when they call in sick to their normal job."

Thomas chuckled. "There you go, Mark. That's a good way to look at it."

"But is that realistic?"

"Sure. Let me give you some examples. We have a whole company that handles entertainment marketing for movie production studios. The people who work there are absolute movie nuts. They know everything there is to know about that business. They attend the events, go to filmings . . . Part of what they get paid to do is watch movies.

"We have another company that is an outdoor outfitter. Every person in that company spends every day dealing with the creation, testing, and distribution of the exact products whose very use helps them fulfill their

Big Five for Life. They get to talk about, play with, test, etc., all the toys they would otherwise be playing with on the weekends."

Mark smiled. "I want those jobs."

Thomas smiled too. "Only if you can tell me how they would help you fulfill your Big Five for Life."

"So this Big Five for Life really is a significant piece of how you run your companies?" Mark asked incredulously.

"You sound surprised."

"Well, it sounds like it would be a lot of work, and certainly out of the comfort zone of most people."

Thomas shook his head, "Not really. Culture rolls downhill, Mark. The Big Five for Life is how I live my life, it's who I am. I started by incorporating it into the interview process, now it's part of our everyday lives. Every person who works with me has their Big Five for Life on the back of their business cards. They have it in their offices; people ask each other about it all the time over the course of everyday discussions. It's not like I force it. People want to talk about their Big Five for Life. They want to fulfill them because they want to be successful as they've defined success. Like I said, they're motivated on their own.

"We even have a Big Five for Life completion wall. Really early on, someone I hired came up with that idea. Now when you walk into our main entryway, there are thousands of pictures and little descriptions people have posted. It's massive at this point."

The camera shifted back to Mark. "Thomas, the two examples you gave, your entertainment-marketing and outdoor-outfitter companies are both in areas where I would think it's easy to find lots of interested employees. What about someone who leads people in an area less exciting."

"You know, I get that question a lot, Mark. First of all, no matter what industry you look at, there are people where the fit would be great and people where the fit would be terrible. There are plenty of people who would hate working in an outdoor-outfitter company.

"I know a lot of city dwellers who couldn't care less about the nuances of kayak construction or backpack frames. And if those people were on top of a mountain for five minutes, they'd be counting the seconds until they could return home. Yet you find companies who hire someone to do promotions for those types of products just because their other skills look like a good fit. The people are really smart, they have great marketing or PR connections. . . . The job requirements and skills of the applicant all match up, but in reality, it's not a good fit at all.

"Well, we don't do that. I want someone who has all of those great attributes *and* has the link to their Big Five for Life. I own fourteen companies, and each of them would seem incredibly exciting to certain people and incredibly boring to others. For every job in every industry, whether it's plumbing supplies, insurance, health care, whatever . . . there are people whose Big Five for Life would be fulfilled by doing that job. You just have to find them. And the motivation that drives you to find them is because when you do, you've got someone who works hard, is self-motivated, and therefore more productive. Add all that together, and it means your company is more profitable."

Mark jumped in as soon as Thomas finished. "Thomas, I see what you mean and I see why it works. But I have to ask again, is it really feasible to believe this can work for *every* leader in *every* company?"

Thomas smiled. "Does it matter?"

Mark looked at him, confused, "What do you mean, does it matter? If I'm a leader out there, I want to know if this can work for me."

"Exactly, Mark. I try not to deal in absolutes when I'm looking for ways to be a better leader—to make my companies more profitable. And as a leader, the question I need to ask is not, can this work for everyone else? I don't care if it can work for everyone else. The question I need to ask is, can it work for *me*? Can it work for *my* company, *my* division, *my* team?"

Thomas smiled. "*Every* is a little more validation than I need to try out an idea, and a little more responsibility than I like to take on, Mark."

Chapter Twenty-nine

I SAT BACK AND WATCHED AS THOMAS AND MARK went back and forth. Mark asked about two of Thomas's other sayings—"Make it a museum day" and "Are you speaking with a stranger." After covering both of those in detail, Mark moved to close the interview.

"Thomas, I want to go back to something and get some specifics from you. As you said, the question a leader should be asking when considering trying to implement something is not 'Can it work for everyone?' but 'Can it work for us.'

"We've talked previously on other shows about how your companies are launched internally; they're homegrown. And then even once they're on their own, they still have many synergistic relationships with all of your other companies. Many of the people watching this interview are leading organizations, divisions, and even departments where they have inherited cultures. They've inherited employees. How realistic is it that they can achieve the type of success you've had, when they're in an environment they didn't have the opportunity to create?"

Thomas took a sip of water from the mug sitting in front of him. "Mark, it all comes back to motivating people. Have you ever gone to a Walt Disney World resort or theme park?"

Mark laughed. "No, I haven't, Thomas."

Thomas smiled. "Well, if you do, you're likely to witness something that in most other settings would seem bizarre."

"The presence of a large animated character?" Mark interjected.

Thomas shook his head. "Well, you may witness that also, but I'm talking about something else. At any given moment, a person in business-dress clothes will be walking from one destination to another and will stop, pick up a piece of paper, a cup, or other piece of trash someone dropped and throw it in a trash can. Executives do it, frontline managers do it, hourly employees do it. Everybody does it.

"There is no special monetary compensation for this behavior. No point system exists where five-dollar bonuses are given out for every fifteen pieces of trash someone picks up. There is also no special monitoring system in place which watches for people who don't do it and then issues penalty points or demerits. Yet, people are motivated to do it anyway.

"Now picking up trash may not be the top concern of your viewers, Mark. But my guess is that as a leader, especially a leader in a division or department they inherited, there are other things they'd like their people to do.

"The good news is they don't need pixie dust or magic. What they do need, though, are some specific steps, which I'll explain."

Thomas paused. "Mark, let me warn you and your viewers in advance. These five steps may seem intimidating. First-time managers, in particular, who were promoted because of their individual skills are often uncomfortable with these ideas. I've run into many of them who come from the perspective that people should do things because 'that's what they get paid to do.' "

"Isn't that the truth?"

"Well, whether it is or isn't, Mark, the fact is money by itself isn't a great long-term motivator. And whether someone *should be* doing something and whether they *are* doing something are two very different things.

"Successful leaders understand that following what I'll share with you enables them to motivate people far beyond what the people get paid for, and far more effectively than when money is the only incentive."

Thomas paused again and took another drink of water. "The first step, Mark, is for the leader to clearly articulate to their people what needs to be accomplished and why. Often the problem with getting people to do things isn't that they're unmotivated, it's that they're uninformed. We've found at our executive seminars that leaders tend to discuss goals with their peers and superiors regularly and are therefore intimately familiar with them. All too often though, because of that familiarity, they mistakenly assume all of their people also know them. Usually, that's not the case.

"Leaders need to take the time to explain to their people exactly what needs to be accomplished and the reasons why. It's important they don't forget the 'Why?' Knowing those pieces of information enables people to make educated choices in their day-to-day decisions. For example, Mark, suppose a team at my media-marketing company is given the goal of launching three new products. Their outputs will vary greatly depending on if their 'Why?' is because their client is losing market share to competitors whose products can be downloaded from the Internet, or because their client wants to break into retail outlets targeting members of the Hispanic community, or because of some other reason.

"And, Mark, if you want to lead people towards a goal, you need to be as specific as possible. I've always been a believer in specific numeric objectives and timelines. A goal of something like 'Improve customer service' is nebulous, and people can't make the best decisions about how to do it or gauge if they're making progress. However, 'Decrease customer wait times to ten seconds by June first' is something people can visualize and work toward."

Thomas smiled. "You know, Mark, I'm sure there are some leaders watching this right now who are thinking, 'Of course, everybody knows that, it's so basic.' And the truth is, I think most leaders do know it, and it is basic."

"But just because they know it doesn't mean they do it," Mark interjected.

"Exactly. Results come from constantly applying what you know, not just knowing."

Mark swiveled in his chair, "Okay, Thomas, that's the first step. What's next?"

"The second step is to involve your people in finding solutions. This can be a tough one for leaders, especially if they have a team with little experience, or if they've historically been rewarded because of their own ability to come up with solutions. The reality, though, is even if the leader can come up with great solutions on their own, they won't get implemented efficiently unless people feel involved. And the best way to get them involved is to let them help create the solution.

"Ideally, Mark, I get my people involved in not only finding solutions for things, but picking the things to find solutions for. I make it a joint effort where the goals for the team are cocreated by all of us.

If that's not possible for a leader, then at a minimum they'd be wise to let their people help create how to achieve the goals. Not only does that generate interest among the group, but study after study has shown you get better solutions this way.

"Successful sports coaches use these techniques all the time, Mark. Sure they watch hours and hours of game films looking for weaknesses in their own team as well as their competitors. But they also involve their players in finding the best way to win. They do it because no matter how much film they watch, or how close they are to the game, they aren't in the game. The perspectives of players or employees who are in the midst of the action can be drastically different from a coach or a manager who is near the action.

"If those perspectives aren't incorporated into the solution, two things will happen. First, those in the midst of the action will feel like no one is listening to them, and so they start to lose interest. Second, decisions will be made without incorporating all the relevant data. Both of these will negatively impact progress toward the goals.

"Speaking of sports, Mark, have you ever played a new sport or game against people who are experienced players?"

Mark nodded. "Sure."

"What is it that can make that experience frustrating?"

Mark laughed. "Well, certainly the fact that everyone else seems to know what they're doing and you don't."

"Exactly. It's pretty typical that every few minutes you do something which you think is correct, only to be told it's illegal, or against the rules. People hate that because it's exceptionally frustrating. So step three is you have to explain the rules of the game to people.

"I meet individual employees and leaders all the time who see the 'frustration' scenario I just mentioned play out in their workplace.

People are given a task, but are not told all the parameters or rules. Weeks into a project they present their work to a senior person, only to be informed they need to change direction because of something they were never told about.

"How demoralizing do you think that is? And think of the costs in terms of people's time, effort, productivity . . . People can find solutions to almost any problem, Mark, but they need to know the rules of the game."

Mark nodded. "Okay, Thomas, that's the first three steps, how about the last two?"

"Step four, Mark, is something we've talked about at length already. You have to link people's personal goals with the organization's goals. In my companies we do it with people's Purpose For Existing, which we also call PFE, and their Big Five for Life. We covered the Big Five for Life a few minutes ago. Purpose For Existing is exactly what it sounds like. It's the reason why something exists. Each of my companies has a clearly defined PFE. And each person who works in my companies has a clearly defined PFE that is aligned with the company's PFE."

"And if it's not?"

"The person wouldn't have gotten hired if it wasn't. In the same way that their responsibilities have to fulfill their Big Five for Life, their Purpose For Existing has to be in alignment with the company's, or we don't extend an offer to them."

Thomas took a sip of his water. "So in terms of this particular step, Mark, leaders need to very regularly make sure what someone is doing every day is somehow linked to both their PFE and the five things they want to do, see, or experience before they die. When a person no longer thinks, 'I work so I can make money,' and instead thinks, 'I work because I love being the one who helps people experience the rush of hang gliding,' there is a significant mental and motivational shift that occurs."

Mark glanced at the producer, who indicated they had just a few minutes left. "Got it, Thomas. Can you give us a quick description of the final step?"

"Sure, Mark, that's easy. This step is particularly important for the leaders you described earlier, who have inherited their people. If for some reason you end up with someone who isn't a good fit, move them off the team right away."

Mark looked surprised. "Really?"

"Really. Nothing halts progress like someone who is either in the wrong spot or discontent simply for the sake of being discontent. It's demoralizing to others and it draws energy and time from the tasks being attempted. You want good counterpoint people on your team. People who say, 'I know what we're all trying to do, and I think there is a better way.' That's valuable in helping make sure the team is on the right track.

"However, someone who just regularly says, 'We'll never get there,' or who has no genuine interest in what they do each day, or what the team is trying to do—they simply hold everyone back. And they're also holding themselves back. You have to move them off the team or they'll destroy the team. Bring in someone whose PFE and Big Five for Life are a good fit for what the team is trying to accomplish; someone who will assist and support the group's efforts."

Mark nodded almost imperceptibly to the producer, who was indicating time was almost over. "Does that ever happen in your companies, Thomas? Where you have to move people off the team?"

"Every once in a while. We've had a few people fake their way through the interview process with the intention of just getting their foot in the door. But it's apparent right away in their productivity that the job they took isn't a good fit with their Purpose For Existing and Big Five for Life."

"And then?"

"We have a very honest and open discussion with them. Then we let them go and encourage them to apply for something that really does fulfill their Big Five for Life and PFE."

"You let them go?"

"We do. How can I speak with integrity to my customers, suppliers, the people who work with me, etc., about the importance of doing something that fulfills you if I don't create a system that supports that?"

"That seems a little harsh, Thomas."

"Actually, Mark, harsh would be forcing the rest of the people to work with that person. There are plenty of opportunities to work in companies where you can lie and do things you don't care about. But not in my companies. Culture rolls downhill, Mark. As a leader, if there's something wrong in one of my companies, it's my fault first."

Thomas smiled. "And you called this the soft skills, Mark."

Mark smiled back. "I know. We're going to have to come up with a different term for it now. And we're going to have to continue this discussion on our next segment, because we are just about out of time."

Mark turned to the camera and it zoomed in on him as he began the wrap-up comments. "We've covered a lot with our guest, Mr. Thomas Derale, President and CEO of Derale Enterprises, and we've got a lot more to come. Join us on our next broadcast, tomorrow at seven p.m. for part two of this three-part series on 'Leadership in the Twenty-first Century.' Tomorrow we'll be discussing the specific business practices Thomas has used to drive his companies to the top of their respective industries. Until then, I'm Mark Whitley, and you're watching *The Business of Business.*"

Chapter Thirty

THE SHOW'S PRODUCER MOVED OUT FROM where he had been crouching near the camera and gave a hand cue to Mark and Thomas, then yelled, "And . . . out. Good job, gentlemen. We'll take a twenty-minute break and tape part two."

The set became a hub of activity as people moved cameras, rearranged lights, and brought script pages up to Mark. Thomas rolled his chair out from behind the desk and Mark patted him on the shoulder. "That was great, Thomas. Take a break and we'll start filming again in about twenty minutes. As I said when I was signing off, let's start the second part with some of your hard-hitting business practices—whatever you want to share. Then we'll see where it goes after that. Do you need anything before we film part two?"

Thomas shook his head. "No, I'm good, Mark. Thanks."

Mark turned away and began consulting with his producer. I watched Thomas stand. He steadied himself against the desk, and I could see he was in significant pain. I got up and started to walk toward him, but he motioned for me to stay where I was, that he would walk to me.

"You look like you're in pain," I said when he got near me.

"Lots of it. It's strange, during the interview I was focused on the interview, but once it ended, the pain kicked in. How did things look from your angle here?"

"Excellent. The content was good, the timing and pace was right on. I couldn't tell at all you were in pain.

"You looked like you," I joked with him. "For what that's worth."

He chuckled. "I'll take that as a compliment."

We talked for about ten minutes regarding the content for the second interview, and then Mark waved Thomas over. They were ready to begin taping again.

"And five, four, three, two . . ." Once again the producer made the gesture to indicate the taping had begun.

"Hello, everyone, and welcome to part two of our three-part series on 'Leadership in the Twenty-first Century.' I'm your host, Mark Whitley, and with me again is our guest, Thomas Derale, founder and CEO of Derale Enterprises. With fourteen highly profitable companies and employees who love him, he clearly has mastered what so many business leaders struggle with. In our last segment he shared with us some of the keys that have made him successful from a people perspective. Today we're going to talk about some of the innovative business practices he employs. Thomas, good to have you back on the show."

"Thanks, Mark, always a pleasure."

"Thomas, companies sometimes gain almost celebrity-like status from stories that seem to be more urban legend than truth. I remember hearing a story about Nordstrom fashion retailer, which is known for their dedication to exceptional customer service. Supposedly, a store manager took a return on a set of automobile tires for a customer, and Nordstrom doesn't even sell tires.

"I've heard a story like that about your companies, Thomas, where customers have been referred to you from an existing client, and you turned them away because you didn't feel you could deliver the type of service you wanted. Where did this story come from, and is there any truth to it?"

Thomas smiled. "First of all, Mark, thanks for the tip on Nordstrom. I've had some tires in my garage for over a year now and could never figure out what to do with them."

Mark laughed. "Time to load them up and go see that guy."

"Seriously though, Mark, I don't know whether that Nordstrom story is true or not, but Nordstrom has clearly created a culture where their leaders are able to focus on giving customers a great experience. True or not, the story demonstrates the genuine spirit of what they're all about. Regarding the story tied to my companies, we have a clear perspective on what we want our customer's experience to be like. Our philosophy is we want every new customer to have the same excellent experience as the person who referred them to us.

"And the truth is, there have been times when because of our own people limitations, system resources, or the resources of one of our partners, we knew we couldn't fulfill that philosophy. In those instances, we turned the customers away."

Mark nodded. "What did you tell them?"

"We explained our philosophy, and the reasons we wouldn't be able to honor it if we took them on. Then we told them how soon it would be before we would be ready to deliver the type of service they had a right to expect, and we insisted on delivering. I think in the first instance it was about six weeks. We were transitioning into a larger space and needed to get everything up and running, and we had hired some new people who weren't done with their training and mentoring. In the midst of all that, we suddenly had four new potential clients who wanted to hire us on."

"So you lost four clients because of your decision?"

"No, actually three of the potential clients said if we could guarantee them we'd be ready in six weeks, they would wait. So we did. We wrote up the contracts, finished everything we needed to do, and then took them on."

"And the fourth one?"

"They went somewhere else. I'd love to tell you they eventually became our client, but I don't think they ever did. And while my people and I don't like losing a potential client, the truth is the loss would have been far greater had we taken them on and then not delivered. Mark, as a company, and as a leader too, you can stand out in people's minds by simply stating what you do, and then doing it.

"For us, that's our minimum definition of success. Most companies don't come anywhere near that. And that gets them in trouble, because you can't maintain your credibility if sometimes you deliver, and other times you don't. What's that famous line from the *Star Wars* movie? The young man is learning from his mentor, Yoda, and Yoda says something along the lines of 'There is no try. There is either do, or don't do, but there is no try.' Well, from our standpoint, if we can't do what we're promising, then we don't make the promise. We either do, or don't do, but we don't try."

Mark nodded. "There's a lot of truth to what you just said, Thomas. You hear more and more stories of disgruntled customers who are receiving subpar service or defective products."

"You're right, Mark, and we don't want any part of our name, or any of our companies, associated with that. You might be able to get some short-term boost to profits that way, but it's a lousy long-term strategy. You lose customer confidence, so your income stream dries up. Good people don't want to work in companies that underdeliver, so they leave, and then your recruiting and training costs skyrocket. And on top of that, your productivity goes down because so many people are new and because you can't get the best people."

"So why do companies do it, Thomas?"

"I think the majority of people have subpar experiences and so they start to believe that's the norm, that it's acceptable. So when those same people are put in leadership positions in their respective companies, they deliver the same subpar performance. They either think subpar is good enough, or they don't know how to deliver better than that.

"Think of it this way, Mark. Suppose you came from Spain and were trying to learn how to speak English. You walk into a room of a thousand English-speaking people. Nine hundred and ninety are from the United States, and ten are from Australia. How likely are you to start talking with someone from Australia?"

"Not very likely."

"Exactly. So after talking with lots of people over the course of the evening, your impression of how to speak English would probably be based on how English is spoken by someone in the United States. As a matter of fact, if someone tried to coach you on how to speak English, and they spoke with an Australian accent, you'd probably tell them they were wrong.

"I think that's the way it goes for people and leadership. They see the way the vast majority of people lead, and then they imitate it. They assume since the majority of the leaders they see are doing things in a similar way, then it must be right. Unfortunately, as you mentioned, the majority of customer experiences, which are a direct result of leadership, aren't so good. So you end up with even more people doing a poor job of leading, which results in even more subpar customer interactions. It becomes a vicious cycle.

"Every once in a while you come across someone or some company who just gets it. The Nordstrom, Starbucks, Southwest Airlines, Google, type companies of the world. They don't do it the way everyone else is doing it. For some reason, they have been able to break out of the mind-set so many other people have."

"And what's the reason?"

"I believe it's the leaders. It starts with one or a small group of leaders who form a company around their own Purpose For Existing, or PFE as I like to call it. It's something that interests them, gets them excited and enthused—something that fulfills them. It's probably part of their Big Five for Life, although they may not have ever heard of that before. Then they grow and attract great leaders so the people in the company have an ongoing stream of role models who, to use my analogy from before, aren't speaking the same old language.

"Instead, these leaders speak a language of having passion for what they do, passion for doing it well, doing what they say not just because it makes smart business sense but because that's who they are. They speak a language where they listen to their customers. And because of all that, their customers rave about them, employees love being a part of their company, and therefore those companies make huge profits."

Mark lifted his hand. "Thomas, do you ever study what's going on in companies who don't speak the language of success?"

"Mark, as you've heard me say many times, leadership flows down-hill. If a company isn't successful, the leader is responsible. This may sound harsh, but personally, I don't spend my time dealing with people or companies who don't speak the language of success. If you're going to focus on the one, choose the right one."

"Focus on the one?"

"Yes, one of the principles I teach all my people, Mark, is to focus on the one. Imagine you're sitting in a hotel room and there's a knock on the door. It's a stranger who tells you they have some great news. A very old, very eccentric relative who you never knew has placed twenty million dollars on the top of Mt. McKinley. The money is in a box that's impossible to open unless you have the key, and the stranger hands you both the key and an airline ticket for a flight heading to Mt. McKinley. The flight leaves in five hours."

Mark laughed. "Sounds good to me."

Thomas smiled at him. "Only one more thing, Mark. The catch is you have to do a rapid ascent of Mt. McKinley to get the money. If you personally don't make it to the top in less than twenty-four hours, you won't get the money. To make matters worse, if you don't get on your flight, or you don't make it to the top in twenty-four hours, or you don't try to make the climb at all, the eccentric old relative has hired a contract killer who will take your life."

Mark laughed again. "Suddenly it doesn't sound as good."

Thomas nodded. "Indeed. So imagine, Mark, there you are with the key and airline ticket, and you decide to go down to the lobby and get some fresh air to think this over. Only you accidentally get off the elevator on the convention floor instead of the lobby. But as luck would have it, directly in front of you is a giant placard announcing the convention in progress is the 'Climb Mt. McKinley' convention.

"As further luck would have it, when you walk in the room, the attendees are split into three groups. The first group is people who tried to climb Mt. McKinley and didn't make it. The second group is people who climbed Mt. McKinley and made it, but it took them more than twenty-four hours, and the third group is people who climbed Mt. McKinley and made it to the top in less than twenty-four hours.

"Your flight leaves in five hours, Mark. Who would you go talk to?"

"The group that made it to the top in less than twenty-four hours."

"Really? You don't want to know what all those other people did? The ones who didn't make it in less than twenty-four hours? You don't want to learn about all the things they did wrong?"

"Not if my life depends on it."

"That's focusing on the one, Mark. We have limited time and energy each day, so why not focus it on learning from the best about how to do whatever it is we want to do, see, or experience. We got on this topic because you asked why those other companies make the decision to adopt a strategy designed for failure. Why they fail to meet their customers' expectations? I don't know. I never study those companies. I study the companies who far exceed their customers' expectations."

Mark held up his hand again. "Thomas, are you suggesting other business leaders don't do that?"

"I'm not suggesting it, Mark. I know it. I was at a speaking conference earlier this year and a panel of meeting planners was going over the top complaints companies had about the speakers they'd brought in to talk about customer service. One of the top complaints was their clients were sick of hearing about Starbucks and Google.

"Now I can see how an audience might become tired of repeatedly hearing high-level information about what those two companies do. But if that was the issue, then the complaint would have been the companies want more specifics, more details. That wasn't the case. They just wanted to hear about somebody else.

"That's not my approach, Mark, and not the approach of my leaders either. In the case of Mt. McKinley and the eccentric relative, your life depends on learning from those who know how to succeed. It's not that different in business, Mark. The timeline may be a little longer, but the truth is, the life or death of a company depends on knowing how to succeed. So we focus on the one, the right one."

Mark nodded as Thomas finished and then shifted some of the papers in front of him. "Thomas, a few years ago when you were on the show, you offered viewers some quick sound-bite-type ideas on ways they could improve their companies. I'd like to spend the last part of this segment doing something similar, only focusing it on leadership. In no particular order, and going with the first things that come to your mind, what brief suggestions can you give leaders watching tonight about being the best leader they can be?"

Thomas paused for a moment. "Sure, Mark. I'll start running through them, you let me know when you've had enough."

Mark nodded. "Go ahead."

"You hear leaders talk about having an open-door policy, Mark, but that's not enough. You can't just have an open door, you need to actually invite people to come in. I have a good friend who was recruited into a management position at a well known financial services company. After a year with them, through no fault of his own, he was in the midst of some serious personal challenges. Family things, a relationship thing . . . A series of these all hit him all at once. He went to his boss and told him he wanted to turn in his resignation. That same day, the senior VP of the division called him and said, 'Let's go to lunch.' She was three levels above him on the organization chart, Mark.

"When they went to lunch, she told him if he wanted to talk about what was going on in his life, she was there to listen. If he didn't, and he just needed time away, that was fine, but she didn't want him to quit. She ended up arranging for him to take six weeks of unpaid leave, during which he left the country, spent some time traveling, and cleared his head. When he came back, the senior VP helped find him a new role, and now he's an executive running one of their divisions.

"That leader stepped up and invited him in, and that's what made the difference. He will never forget what she did, and it impacts everything he does for the company, from the way he performs his everyday responsibilities all the way through to things like campus recruiting."

Thomas cleared his throat and paused for a moment. "Here's another idea, Mark, totally unrelated to the story I just shared. Each year, from the very first year I started my initial company, we dedicate time during our slow period to identify and eliminate the ten percent most annoying and time-consuming tasks we do. We nominate them, measure them, and then either find a way to get rid of them or find a better way to do them.

"There are two ways for a leader to impact profits. You either boost your revenue or decrease your costs. This one helps us decrease our costs, and it constantly improves morale, because we're always getting rid of the least enjoyable parts of people's responsibilities. It's like a spring cleaning every year and has yielded some huge results for us."

Mark smiled. "I like that. How about a few more, Thomas."

"Alright. This applies to all leaders, but especially to those who deal with customers. On a regular basis, put yourself in your customer's shoes and see what it's like to interact with your own company. Let me give you two brief examples. My wife, Maggie, and I were in Bali on vacation. We had a wonderful time, it was an amazing week, and then at the airport as we were leaving, they imposed an exit tax of almost seventy dollars per person on each of us. When we had arrived, there was no indication we would have to pay an exit tax, so we had spent every last Balinese dollar we had, and now we needed one hundred and forty more U.S. dollars' worth of them.

"We ended up having to change money with the government money-changing service right at the airport, which offered a much lower exchange rate than everyone else. And, they refused to exchange any U.S. currency that had a date on it more than five years old.

"Honestly, Mark, up until that experience I didn't even realize U.S. paper money had a date on it. What amazed me about the entire process was how shortsighted the leader was who created it. Why would you ever create something that guarantees your customer's final impression of you will be negative? Even if we hadn't had to go through the money-changing debacle, just the fact that they were charging people to leave was ridiculous. If they would have charged everyone to enter, people might have grumbled, but after spending an amazing vacation in Bali—which is truly a spectacular place—they would have forgotten about it by the time they were leaving. This way it was the last thing they remembered. Not smart.

"The other example is something I noticed recently. Some airlines are now charging a ten-dollar booking fee, even when the customer books the ticket themselves over the Internet."

Mark laughed. "They're charging a booking fee to people who book their own ticket?"

Thomas nodded. "I know, Mark, think of how illogical that is, but it's true. The airlines are in the business of moving passengers, and then they charge the passenger an extra fee when the passenger does the work the airline should be doing in the first place. That would be like a bank charging you a fee each time you have funds direct-deposited into your own account.

"Leaders are the ones responsible for looking at those types of things and realizing the degree to which they both alienate customers and also just don't make sense. If you want the extra ten dollars, roll it into the price of the ticket, but creating ill will like they've done with the booking fee is bad business. And that means there's bad leadership somewhere."

As Thomas was finishing, the producer gave a signal to Mark, indicating five minutes remained.

Mark nodded slightly in the direction of the producer and turned to Thomas. "We've got about five minutes left, Thomas. Do you have one or two more sound-bite-type suggestions for our viewers looking to become better leaders?"

"Fear leads to failure, and fearless leads to success, Mark. If I do something great in my company, that's just one leader doing something great. If I have dozens or hundreds of leaders doing great things, that's way more than I could ever do on my own. I teach my people everything I know, and I teach them to be fearless. Will they fail every once in a while? Sure, and that's okay. And I tell them that it's okay.

"When you push beyond mediocrity towards greatness, you're going to trip now and again. People who succeed in their journey understand that. They also understand falling down only becomes a problem if you don't get back up. At its core, fear is a product of a lack of experience, or a lack of knowledge. When you lack neither, fear goes away.

"Unfortunately, a lot of leaders out there hoard their knowledge and the opportunities for their people to gain the right experiences."

"Why is that?" Mark asked.

"Mostly, it's ego and insecurity. Some leaders like the power rush of being the 'go-to person,' the one who knows all the answers. They feel important and valuable when everyone has to come to them in order to get something done. And if that's what makes them happy, fine by me. It's an incredibly ineffective way to lead, though. The truly successful leaders—the ones who excel on all fronts and for long durations—are the ones who get a rush by seeing their people grow to the point where they can do what needs to be done on their own.

"Think of it this way, Mark. You're a parent in New York City and you want your kids to learn how to get around town on the subway. Is it more effective to insist you buy their ticket each time, and you tell them which train to take and which stop to get off at, or do they learn more by you letting them do those things?"

Mark laughed. "As a parent who has raised two kids in New York City, I can tell you from personal experience it is far more effective to teach *them* than to go with them everywhere they want to go."

"And how did you do it?"

Mark shrugged. "It was easy really. I showed them how to buy tickets, and then let them buy them. I had them show me where we were on the map and tell me when we needed to get off. I even let them go past the stop we needed a few times so they would learn how to backtrack if they missed their stop. My goal was to let them make mistakes in a safe environment while I was there, so when I wasn't there, I'd know they could figure it out."

"Exactly," Thomas replied. "And the impact of that goes way beyond just the New York subway. Once you've taught them to navigate, how afraid are they going to be when they need to do the same thing on the subway in Rome, Tokyo, Beijing . . . ? How afraid are they when they need to figure out a train or a bus schedule? You laid the foundation for them to be successful, and because of that, they can keep building upon it. In the same way you helped your kids become strong, confident individuals, a great leader helps their people become strong, confident leaders."

The producer flashed three fingers at Mark.

"Thomas, we've got time for one more quick one. What have you got?"

Thomas smiled. "Lead like Tiger Woods learned to play golf."

Mark laughed. "What?"

"Mark, I remember reading that when he was three years old, Tiger Woods got his first par. By the time he was five or six, he was consistently hitting the ball better than most adults ever do. It wasn't because he was swinging harder than most adults. He was swinging the club smarter. He was optimizing his output compared to his input.

"From the first day I started my company, I've stressed that our success would be built not on working harder, but on working smarter, and more effectively. I don't want a situation where my people are working until seven or eight p.m. every night, because that's the only way we can get everything done. If they love what they're working on and just feel like working on it one night, that's their call. But no way should they be there because otherwise it won't get done.

"Maggie and I have a friend named Diane, who works at a large corporation near us. I remember one time where we hadn't seen each other in a few months, and Diane called us to schedule a dinner. We were supposed to meet at six thirty p.m. She called at four thirty and asked if we could push it to eight p.m. Then she called again at seven to push it to nine. Finally, at eight thirty she called to say it just wasn't going to happen. This was a dinner she booked with us, mind you.

"A few weeks later, the three of us eventually met up for lunch, and do you know what, Mark? When I asked her, she couldn't even remember what the crisis had been the night she'd had to cancel her own dinner. Apparently, practically every night was a crisis. It was common for a senior person to make a sudden request which would cause all the directors and managers to scramble to put something together by the next day. When she thought about it for a while, she concluded what she and her team had worked on—what her leader had conveyed as so incredibly important that it had to be done that night—was left unused and probably unopened.

"What do you think that did to her morale, Mark? And that's just her. She'll be the first to tell you much of their company operates that way. Which means the behavior is being driven by someone at the top of the organization.

"Great leaders lead know it's not about working longer. It's about working smarter, so you're always getting the maximum result for the minimum amount of effort."

Mark smiled. "Another great example, Thomas, and another great show. I know the content you shared today will be a great asset to a lot of leaders out there." Mark turned to face the camera. "What you've been watching is part two of our three-part series on 'Leadership in the Twenty-first Century.' Join us . . .'"

Chapter Thirty-one

WHEN WE ARRIVED HOME FROM THE STUDIO, maggie was there to greet Thomas and me. She wrapped her arms around Thomas and gave him a long kiss. "How is my celebrity husband?"

He pulled her close and she laid her head against his chest. He held her there for a long time. Then he kissed her on the top of the head. "I love you," he said.

She squeezed him tight. "I love you too."

After a few moments, Maggie pulled her head away from his chest, looked up at him, and smiled. "So, how did it go today?"

Thomas smiled back. "Better ask Joe. He could see how it looked from the audience."

"It went well, Maggie," I said. "Your man was on his game."

"When does it air?" she asked.

Thomas put down his cane and sat on the nearest chair. "We taped two shows. They'll air those tonight and tomorrow, then call us back about when we'll tape the third one. It will be sometime the day after tomorrow, I just don't know exactly when."

* * *

THOMAS, MAGGIE, and I arrived at the television studio at 6:30 p.m. It was the night after the second episode had aired. Mark had called Thomas at home after the second show was on and told him the viewer response to the first two episodes had been so good, they wanted to do the third show live from the Chicago studio. It was the first time in the show's history they would do a live show from somewhere other than where they normally shot in New York.

"All set to go, Thomas?" Mark asked as we walked onto the set.

"Whenever you are, Mark," Thomas replied. He introduced Mark to Maggie, and then she and I went and sat down.

The makeup and sound people worked with Thomas for a few minutes, getting him ready for the show. At 6:57, everyone left the set, leaving Mark and Thomas in front of the cameras.

Mark smiled at Thomas when the show's producer called out, "Two minutes to air." "Just like the other day, Thomas. Only this time millions of people are watching live."

Thomas smiled back. "Don't worry, Mark, I'll cover for you in case you forget something."

Mark laughed, and in a minute the producer counted down "Five, Four, Three, Two . . . ," and they were live.

"Good evening, ladies and gentlemen, and welcome to *The Business of Business*. My name is Mark Whitley, and this is the third of our three-part series on 'Leadership in the Twenty-first Century.' My guest once again is the founder, CEO, and Chairman of the Board of Derale Enterprises, Mr. Thomas Derale. You are in for a rare treat tonight. Normally when we do interviews at off-site locations, we tape the show and air it the same day. Because of the overwhelming response to the first two segments of this series, we made the decision to run this third segment live from our sister studio here in Chicago, Illinois. What you will see tonight is live and without edits."

Mark introduced Thomas and then gave a brief overview of what they had talked about on the previous two shows.

"Thomas, I want to switch directions a little bit tonight. Many great people talk about defining moments—instances in their lives where something happened that set them on a particular path, or where they learned something that completely turned the world around for them. Can you share with us a few of your own personal defining moments and how they've shaped your views on leadership?"

Thomas paused for a few seconds. "Mark, I've got a few that come to mind instantly. Why don't we start with those and you tell me when you've had enough."

"Okay."

"Very early in my career I was working in an entry-level business job at a university. I had gone to college and trained to become an airline pilot. Unfortunately I got hurt and, because of the injury, couldn't fly anymore. So at twenty-two years of age, I went through the classifieds and applied for this job. During the interview process I met Walter, the guy who would be my boss. We talked for about an hour or so, and he seemed pretty normal. A few months into the job, though, it was apparent he was far from normal. This guy was an egomaniac, a micromanager, and a manipulator, who did his best to rule by fear."

"Sounds like a real treat to have as a boss," Mark commented.

"Exactly. He was in charge of almost one hundred employees, and he was constantly berating and belittling them. And on top of that, he constantly made derogatory and completely inappropriate sexist comments about the capabilities of women.

"Each week, his regular practice was to make a giant schedule indicating when people could take their lunches and breaks. Then he'd spend the vast majority of his day checking to make sure people went exactly when he'd told them they could and that they were back within their allotted time.

"One afternoon he came into the office I shared with two other guys, and he went on an absolute tirade. He was literally in the face of every one of us because we had sent off a report and had only put the department name on it, and not his name. Apparently he was trying to impress the person who had requested this particular report, and so despite its being typical to send out hundreds of reports with just the department name, he wanted his name on this one.

"That day wasn't the first time he had acted like this, but it was the most vicious. His attack wasn't just unmerited and ludicrous, it was personal. That day I made the decision I'd had enough. The next morning I called the head of the human resources department for the university and asked to meet about a transfer to somewhere else. I walked to his office that afternoon during my lunch hour—"

"The hour your boss had scheduled for you," Mark interjected with a smile.

"Of course. So I walked there, and when we met, I explained what the situation was and why I wanted to transfer. I made a point of getting his agreement that our conversation would remain confidential, because I knew Walter would go on another tirade if he knew I was asking to leave because of his behavior. I was assured the conversation would remain confidential and that he would see what he could do about a transfer.

"It took me twenty minutes to walk across the campus back to where I worked. When I arrived, there was a note on my desk from Walter—'I need to see you immediately!' So much for confidentiality. The guy I'd met with had called him as soon as I'd walked out of his office. Walter went on another tirade, insisting to know exactly what I had told this guy. It wasn't pretty."

Mark shook his head in amazement. "What ended up happening?"

"I took a transfer and then left the university soon after that. It was a terrible experience, but at the same time it was a defining moment, because at twenty-two years of age it gave me firsthand experience with what really bad leadership was. I learned there was no point in working for a lousy leader. They don't value quality people. Instead, they're intimidated by them. How are you going to grow and get promoted in that environment?

"I also saw that lousy leaders are bad for a company's profitability. Because of Walter's behavior, the department I worked in was constantly losing people and having to hire new ones. Good people don't stick around and work for lousy leaders, so you either end up with a rotating group of talented new hires who quickly quit, or marginal employees who do marginal work. Either way, it results in low productivity and average output, both of which are bad for profits.

"And, I learned using fear is an ineffective way of leading. It can generate really short-term results, but again, talented people don't stick around in that type of environment, and people who are always afraid of making mistakes become completely ineffective. They end up so afraid of making the wrong decision that they either make no decisions, or the fear clouds their judgment so much they make even more mistakes."

Mark shook his head. "Thomas, that's an amazing story. Do you want to elaborate further with that experience, or do you have a few other defining moments you want to share?"

"I could elaborate more, Mark, including how that taught me the importance of having quality people leading the human resources efforts, but let's move on. That experience was sort of the anti-mentor. I learned a lot about what not to do, and how not to lead. The story I'll share with you now really hit me in terms of the importance of a great mentor.

"I'd been running my company for a number of years and was looking for a way to explain something I call the ripple effect of leadership."

"The ripple effect?"

"Right, it's where one event happens, which then leads to another event, which leads to still another, and all of them have their origin with that single event."

"Sort of like the old analogy that a butterfly flaps its wings in one place and eventually there's a typhoon somewhere else," Mark said.

Thomas nodded. "Exactly. Only in this case, I was looking for a good example of how powerful the impact can be when someone fulfills their Purpose For Existing and Big Five for Life. Interestingly enough, I found my example on an Oprah Winfrey show."

"Really?"

"Yes, really." Thomas glanced to where Maggie and I were sitting near the cameras and smiled at her. "I was lucky in that my wife has been an *Oprah* fan for a long, long time and often tapes the show. I had shared with her I was looking for this ripple effect example, and after watching this one particular *Oprah* show, she told me I 'had to see it.' And sure enough, she was right."

Mark smiled. "You've got my interest piqued, Thomas. What was on the show?"

"Actually it wasn't a what, it was a who. Oprah invited the singer Diana Ross to the show, and during the interview Oprah shared how when she was a young girl, she had seen Diana Ross singing on television, and it had changed her life. She said she remembered watching her and thinking to herself, 'I want to be like that. I want to be like *that*.'

"As I watched the show, it struck me that if Diana Ross hadn't followed her passion and fulfilled what I would imagine is her Purpose For Existing, then maybe Oprah Winfrey never would have had that moment of inspiration. Perhaps without that moment, without that role model, Oprah wouldn't have seen in herself all the potential that was there. If that didn't happen, perhaps she wouldn't have ended up pursuing a career in television, and owning her own show, now her own network.

"And if all of that hadn't happened, then millions upon millions of people wouldn't have gotten inspired the way they have because of what she's done. Not just from her show, but also from all the shows she has produced through her network.

"And if you take it back a step further, I wonder who it was in Diana Ross's life who inspired her to believe in herself. Who encouraged her to follow that calling she had inside herself to sing? Because without that person, perhaps Diana Ross would never have been on TV, and so of course Oprah couldn't have seen her. So in some way, that person who inspired Diana Ross is also partly responsible for enabling the millions upon millions of people to be inspired through Oprah.

"That's what I mean by the ripple effect. The point I make with my people, is when they make the decision to be a great leader, the impact of their actions will extend well beyond anything they will ever know. They will be a role model not only for the people who they interact with directly, but to some degree, their actions have the potential to positively impact people for generations. That's a powerful realization, Mark. It enables leaders to see the true scope of their actions, and I believe in the people I've led, it has been one of the things that most inspires them to pursue greatness, versus mediocrity."

Mark nodded. "Another powerful story, Thomas. What struck me as you were sharing that is not only do leaders have the chance to have a positive impact for generations, but it they lead poorly, the effects of their leadership can have a negative impact for generations."

"Without a doubt, Mark. I remind my people of that as well."

"Do you have one more for us, Thomas?"

Thomas nodded. "I do. What I'm about to share with you was taught to me at a critical juncture in my life. I won't give you all the details, because the message is more important than how I came to learn it. Suffice it to say, though, the man who taught me this forever changed my life for the better.

"You and I were just talking about the ripple effect. I doubt he knows the degree to which what he taught me has changed the life of many, many people. But it certainly has. I've passed this on to every person who has ever worked with me, and I know the lesson has cascaded from there.

"The essence of it is really quite simple. When this man shared it with me, he began with a single question: 'Would you like to live four more lives?'

Mark looked at Thomas inquisitively. "Four more lives?"

"Yes, that's what he asked me. And like you right now, I looked at him a little confused. Then he broke it down for me in a very simple fashion. He explained that most people spend about ten hours per day, five days per week, at a job they don't like. They do things that if they weren't paid to do them, they wouldn't. They tolerate work as an accepted exchange of hours of their life for dollars they can spend.

"By the time they've commuted home and eaten dinner, what they're left with is approximately two and a half hours of time in which they can participate in whatever they actually *like* to do. The things they do not because they get paid for them, but because they just like to do them.

" 'Imagine,' he told me, 'if you became a leader who created a place where people got paid to do the things they like. A place people were proud to be a part of, because of what that place stood for. A place where every day they felt like their efforts were meaningful and important. Now, instead of living just one life of approximately twelve and a half meaningful hours each workweek, the fifty hours of life they'd be spending at work would become meaningful too. Now they're living four extra lives.' "

Mark nodded his head. "Interesting concept."

"Interesting and effective. I mentioned earlier that we only bring people into our company whose personal Purpose For Existing is in line with the organization's PFE. And only then if their Big Five for Life are somehow fulfilled by what they will be doing at their job every day. People who work with me don't just get a paycheck, Mark. They get a paycheck, they get progress toward their Big Five for Life so their life is a success as they define success, and they get four extra lives."

Mark laughed. "That's a tough one to pass up, Thomas. And what do you get in return?"

"I doubt it will surprise you to hear it, Mark, but when you provide people with all of that, they *do more* for you, they *are more* for you, and they work harder for you than you can possibly imagine. So we get great results. Since my company's Purpose For Existing is based on my personal Purpose For Existing, those great results mean my own PFE is being fulfilled."

Mark nodded. "Alright, Thomas, how about one more defining moment."

Thomas paused for a few seconds. "Mark, I remember one of the first executive summits I was asked to speak at. I shared the concept of Purpose For Existing and the Big Five for Life, and the way we were using them. Afterwards, one of my good friends who was attending the event came up to me. He and I had known each other for a long time socially, but never in a business context. He said he really loved the techniques, but could never share them with his employees because he was afraid they would all leave."

Mark smiled. "I think there are some viewers who might be thinking the same thing, Thomas. What did you do?"

"Well, Mark, I remember thinking to myself—his people have already left. If they are that poised to flee, think of how unproductive they must be every day. And if they are that unhappy, how must they be treating the customers? His company had been slowly growing over the last decade and was profitable each year. With that type of environment, though, he had to have been leaving the vast majority of the profits on the table. His business was succeeding in spite of itself.

"That interaction struck me as so significant because this guy was a smart person, and a good guy. It wasn't that he didn't want his people to be happy, and it wasn't that he didn't care about making profits in his company."

"What did you tell him, Thomas?"

"I told him I thought he was shorting himself and shorting his people. Mark, every company has a Purpose For Existing. It may not be clear to everyone in the company, but there is a reason why every company exists. I challenged him to think about what the PFE was for his company. Out of all the things he could have done, why did he start that company? Out of all the things he could be doing now, why did he want that company to exist?

"If the answer was simply to make money, fine. If the answer was something else, fine. But whatever it was, I challenged him to figure it out. Because his people wanted to know it, his customers wanted to know it, and everyone else who interacted with his company wanted to know it. And until they did, he'd be realizing a fraction of his company's true potential. And therefore, he'd be realizing a fraction of the company's potential profitability."

Mark looked at Thomas. "And what happened?"

"Nothing."

"Nothing?"

"He never did it. Most people don't, Mark."

"But why? You said he knows you. He obviously knows your track record. Plus he's the head of the company and therefore has a lot to gain. You would think he would want to at least explore the idea if it meant that much more potential profitability. Why didn't he do it?"

"Why are the 'Wash your hands after going to the bathroom' signs on the mirrors, Mark?"

"What?"

"When you go into the men's room in a restaurant—I assume it's in the women's too, but I know it's in the men's bathroom because I've seen thousands of them. On all the mirrors they have those signs that say, 'Employees must wash hands before returning to work.'"

Mark laughed. "I've always thought that practice should be obvious to people."

"Me too, but that's not the point. The point is, where are those signs? The vast majority of the time they're on the mirror, positioned right above the sink. Now if you're already standing at the sink looking at the mirror, odds are you're already washing your hands. It's fine to have the sign there too, but wouldn't it be far more effective if there were signs on top of the urinals, on the back of the stall doors, and right next to the handle of the exit door. But there aren't, Mark. Why not?"

Mark laughed again. "I don't know. Why not?"

"For the same reason my friend didn't ever stop to figure out his companies PFE. Most of the time people just do what they've seen everyone else do. They lead like every one else, they run their companies like everyone else, and they put their bathroom signs in the same spot as everyone else. Not because it's the most effective way to do things, not because it's the most profitable way to do things, but because it's easier to follow everyone else than to think about why they're doing what they're doing. And it's definitely easier to do that than to change."

Chapter Thirty-two

MARK AND THOMAS DISCUSSED TWO MORE brief concepts, and then I saw the producer give Mark a signal that they had just a few minutes left.

"Thomas, you've been a great guest, and it's been a pleasure having you on the show for all three segments. We've got just a few minutes left. Do you have a final concept or final story you want to leave our viewers with?"

Thomas took a few moments before answering. "I'll tell you what, Mark. Why don't I share with you one of life's greatest secrets, which is also one of the greatest secrets of leadership. Then I'll close with a story."

Mark nodded. "Alright, Thomas, what's the secret?"

Thomas took a piece of paper and drew a small diagram. Then he held it up for the camera.

"For most people, this is how they go through life, Mark. On the X axis is time, and on the Y axis is satisfaction with life. And this basic sine curve—the up-and-down lines that looks like little hills and valleys—it represents their life. Over the course of their life, people have highs, and they have lows. But in general, their highs are about the same high, and their lows are about the same low. They just oscillate between these two points.

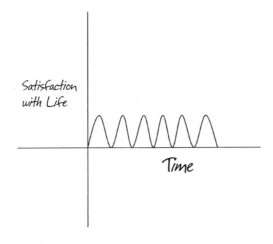

"The secret to life, Mark, is to have a sine curve that doesn't just go on over time, but that ascends over time. I call it an ascending life curve. And it looks like this." Once again, Thomas made a little diagram and held it up for the camera.

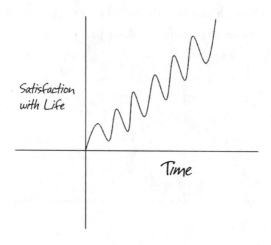

"You see, in this person's life, as time goes by, they don't just oscillate between a set of highs and lows, but they keep reaching new highs. Everybody has lows, Mark. It happens. Even when you're on the right journey, and heading in the direction you want to go, there are still lows. You may be heading off to the Hawaiian vacation of your dreams, but even on those trips the plane gets delayed every once in a while, or they show in-flight movies you've already seen.

"But the point is, Mark, when you're on an ascending life curve, at some moment in time your lows are now higher than what used to be your highs. And the way to do that is actually very simple, Mark. The more moments of your day you spend on something that fulfills your Purpose For Existing, and the more moments each day you spend on your Big Five for Life, the more your life curve ascends.

"Being a successful leader is simple, Mark. You just need to know this secret." Thomas tapped on the diagrams he had just explained. "And then you need to apply it. You bring people into your organization whose PFE is in alignment with the organization's. You put people in positions where they get to fulfill their Big Five for Life simply by doing the job the company needs done each day. And you teach them to do the same for the people they lead.

"When you do that, you're helping people's life curve ascend, Mark. And in the process they're helping the organization's life curve ascend. Because just like a person, an organization has a life curve too. For me, when the life curves of the organization, *and* the people in the organization, are ascending—that's the sign of a great leader."

Thomas looked into the camera. His voice paused and grew full of emotion. "Mark, as you know . . . and as those close to me know . . . I'm dying." Thomas paused again. "We all are really, I just happen to be in the unique position where I know about how much time I have left . . . and it's very little. A long time ago I learned something which has been an important part of who I am. It's an important part of the way I've led, and how I've tried to inspire my own leaders to lead. It's something that makes me okay with the fact that my life is coming to a close. If it's alright with you, that's the story I'd like to close with."

I looked at Mark. He appeared a little surprised. I don't think he knew exactly where Thomas was heading, and it had caught him a bit off guard. After a brief moment of unexpected silence on his part, he said, "That's fine, Thomas. Your call. Whatever you'd like."

Thomas nodded. When he began speaking, his voice was smooth and confident, yet almost quiet in a way. "Mark, more than twenty years ago my wife and I took almost a year off from everything else, and we backpacked around the world. It was something we had both wanted to do for a long time, and despite the thousands of reasons why it couldn't be done, or why it wasn't the ideal time, we just said, 'That's it, we're doing it.' Five weeks after making the decision, we were standing on a tiny street in Bangkok, Thailand, at the start of our journey. As that journey progressed, it became more and more apparent how much the experiences we were having meant to me. I understood why I had felt such a calling to embark on the exact adventure we were living.

"After seven and a half months of being on the road, we were in Africa. The trip had already changed my life dramatically. It was about to be changed even more in just a few days. See, I had dreamed of seeing the African animals ever since I was a small child. And for seven straight days we camped in the midst of them. We saw thousands of elephants, rhinoceros, giraffes, zebras . . . They were so close that at times we could have reached out and touched them. We saw a baby giraffe be born and we saw lions kill. . . . For me, it was the pinnacle of all the amazing experiences we'd had during our seven and a half months of travel.

"The morning we were leaving, I woke up early and was lying in our little A-frame tent. And the thought that came to me, the realization I had, was I could die right then and I would be okay with that. I didn't want to die, but I had seen so much, and fulfilled so much of what I had dreamt about, that if my life were to end, I'd feel like I had lived the life I was born to live."

Thomas paused and I glanced around the studio. Every person—those manning the cameras, the set people, the producers—all of them were watching Thomas. The studio was completely absent of not just sound, but of motion too.

"When my wife, Maggie, woke up, we packed our camping gear and rolled up our tent and got on the road. About thirty minutes into our travels, she turned to me and said, 'I had the strangest thought this morning. I woke up and thought with all we've seen and done during our trip . . . I could die today . . . and I'd be okay with that.'"

"Wow," Mark said softly, in an almost unintentional exclamation.

Thomas looked at him. "It was wow, Mark. It still is wow for me, even after all these years. And what I took away from that moment has been one of the greatest keys to success in my life and my success as a leader.

"Always write the ending first, Mark. Always write the ending first. Start with life, so you can create an existence where one day—hopefully soon—you wake up and you honestly feel if you died that day, you'd be okay with it. Not that you want to die, but if you did, you've gotten to a place where you could die with no regrets.

"Now it may sound trite compared to an overall life, but then learn to write the ending first in other things too. I learned from my experience that morning to write the ending first in everything I did. What kind of company did I want to build? What kind of leaders did I want to create? What type of relationship did I want my wife and I to have on our tenth anniversary?

"I made it such a part of my life that even little things, like a meeting, I'd ask myself, 'What does the ending look like? What do I want to have achieved? How do I want to feel? How do I want the other people in the room to feel?'"

Thomas lowered his eyes for a moment and let out a small sigh. "Mark, life goes by quickly. I can't believe I've been alive for fifty-five years. In some ways it seems like I just arrived, and yet the truth is . . . my journey here is almost over. We either write the ending we want, and then create a life that gets us there, or we end up living someone else's story, and having an ending that pales compared to the one we would have written for ourselves. . . . It's really that simple."

Thomas finished speaking and the cameras swung back to Mark. He had clearly been affected by what had just happened. For a few moments he said nothing. When he began speaking, his face and voice were full of emotion.

"Ladies and gentlemen, it is a rare moment as a broadcaster that something surprises you, touches you, changes the way you look at your life . . ." He paused and looked up into the camera. "Makes you a better person than you were when the show began. . . . This has been one of those times. As you heard him say, Thomas Derale is dying. Because of his declining health, this is the last time he will be on this show . . . this has been our last chance to spend time with him. And that, ladies and gentlemen, is a tremendous loss for all of us.

"This has been a very special edition of *The Business of Business*. . . . My name is Mark Whitley. Good night, everyone."

Chapter Thirty-three

AS THE CAMERAS STOPPED ROLLING AND THE set came alive, my cell phone vibrated. It was Sonia.

"Hey, Sonia."

"Joe, I was watching the show. That was amazing. Absolutely amazing. Everything came together for me tonight. All the things we talked about on the plane, everything I saw at the MMB session. Everything Thomas has created was designed to help people have an ascending life curve. And not just to have one, but to have a steep one so their life was getting better and better as quickly as possible."

I smiled at Sonia's enthusiasm. "It was a pretty amazing show," I replied. "You should see what's happening here. As we speak, Thomas is being mobbed on the set by people who usually go right from the end of filming a show to whatever their next task is. He touched some people's lives tonight."

THE NEXT morning I walked into the kitchen and found Maggie sitting at the table. I gave her a hug. "Good morning, Maggie."

She smiled and hugged me back. "Good morning, Joe."

"How's Thomas?"

"He's still sleeping. I turned off the phone. It's been ringing nonstop since the show last night. I spoke with Kerry Dobsin this morning. She said from when the show ended until this morning, seventy-two thousand people have filled out the online application for Derale Enterprises, including putting down their PFE and Big Five for Life. She also said the phone lines have been busy nonstop with people who want to do business with Thomas."

I smiled. It was the final validation of everything Thomas practiced as a leader.

"Kerry asked if you would call her. Apparently the phone lines are also ringing off the hook with media inquiries. She wondered if you'd be willing to help handle some of them. She also wants to talk with you about something else . . . something she and I have been working on."

I smiled again. "Sounds secretive."

She smiled back. "It is. You'll understand once you talk with her."

Chapter Thirty-four

THOMAS SLEPT ALMOST NONSTOP IN THE DAYS immediately following the last television interview. In a strange twist of his disease, his pain went away, but extreme fatigue seemed to overtake him. For almost a week, he and I talked little. At the end of that week he had another seizure and had to be rushed to the hospital again.

He was there for three days, and during that time, his condition took a dramatic turn for the worse. The fatigue only partially went away, and the pain came back in force. Despite his doctors' efforts and the prayers and well wishes of so many, it was apparent the end of his life was coming soon. The tumor now impacted his equilibrium so much it was impossible for him to maintain his balance for more than a few steps. When he returned home from the hospital, it was in a wheelchair. That would be how he got from place to place from now on.

One morning shortly after his return home, the phone rang. It was Kerry Dobsin. Thomas, Maggie, and I were all sitting at the table on the patio, so Maggie put the call on the speakerphone.

"Thomas, I hate to ask this, but I need your help and I need it in person. I know you just got out of the hospital, but can you come down to the company headquarters tomorrow at one? It's important."

I glanced at Thomas as he leaned toward the speaker. He looked tired. "Can you tell me what it's about, Kerry?"

"Not cohesively over the phone, Thomas. It's in regard to the expansion project, but it's one of those things where I have to show you where we're at and see if you can figure out the best way to take it where we want to go. I've been at it for days, as has the team, but we just can't seem to get by a few key points, and it's holding up the project. I wouldn't have called, but we're really stumped on this one, and we need to get past it by end of day tomorrow or it's going to delay the entire project for another few months because of permitting issues. We need *you* for this one, Thomas."

"Okay, hang on." Thomas turned to Maggie. "Are you busy tomorrow afternoon? Can you drive me to the office?"

Because Thomas was now using a wheelchair, he had rented a special van instead of using a car service. Maggie and I had been taking turns as the driver.

Maggie thought for a moment. "I've got some appointments from ten to about two thirty, but I'll be back after that. I can change them if you want."

I motioned to Thomas. "I can take you. My whole day is open."

Thomas leaned toward the speaker again. "Okay, Kerry, I'll see you at one. Call me if something comes up and you need me there earlier."

* * *

THE NEXT day, Thomas and I had lunch at his house. It took everything I had to contain the giant smile that kept spreading across my face. I wanted this to be a surprise. Ever the judge of character, Thomas took one look at me and said, "You are in a particularly good mood this morning, Joe. What's up?"

"I'm always in a good mood, Thomas, you know that."

"Uh-huh," he replied, and smiled. "You just keep your secret to yourself then."

Despite his smile, Thomas looked drawn and tired. He'd kept himself in good shape throughout his entire life. Now, because of the tumor, he'd lost almost thirty pounds, and he looked painfully thin.

We arrived at his company headquarters just before one. As I helped Thomas from the car and into his wheelchair, an involuntary groan of pain escaped his lips.

"Sorry, Thomas," I said.

"That's alright, Joe. It's not you."

I helped him get situated in the wheelchair and started to push him toward the entrance to his company. After a few steps, I glanced down at him and saw something amazing. He was changing. With each step I took in pushing his chair toward his company's entrance, his features seem to come back a little. He looked a little more like himself.

As we neared the front door, it opened and Josephine came out. She smiled and gave Thomas a long hug in his chair. "Good to have you back, Thomas. Kerry mentioned you were coming in for a meeting. I've been looking forward to it all day."

Thomas returned her hug. "It's good to be back, Josephine. And good to see things are still in good hands."

Josephine closed the door behind us as I rolled Thomas into the lobby. "Kerry said for you to meet her by the expansion-project office. With all that work they're doing, things have been getting moved around quite a bit. But if you go through the hall here and take a left at the new doorway at the end, you'll find her. As a matter of fact, why don't I walk you down. It will just take a minute."

I rolled Thomas down the short hallway and to the large glass double doors. They were still covered in the brown paper the contractors had affixed to prevent them from being painted or cracked during the construction. When we were just a few feet away from the doors, they swung open into a large two-story entryway that had offices on either side. The entire length of the entryway was filled with people. They were seven and eight deep on both sides, and when the doors opened, they began to cheer and laugh and shout and applaud.

As I rolled Thomas down the hall, the cheering got louder. The wide entryway curved to the right, and as we came around the corner, the noise became even louder. When I was younger, I had attended some of the Chicago Bulls games at the old Chicago Stadium when Michael Jordan was bringing his first championship to the city. I'd never heard anything like the pandemonium when they would announce the starting lineup and get to Jordan. Up until now that was. This was deafening.

In front of us was a brand-new atrium. It was five stories tall and elegantly designed with an all-glass dome and all-glass front. The plants and fountains in the interior made it feel like a remote tropical paradise. Or it would have felt like that except there were literally thousands of people inside. All of them were cheering for Thomas. They flanked a red carpet that went from the side entrance where we'd entered the atrium and ended at a giant curtain on the other side. I looked up at the balconies on each side of the atrium. Every one of the four floors above us was packed multiple layers deep with cheering people.

Josephine leaned down and hugged Thomas again. She smiled at him and started to cry. "They're all here for you, Thomas. . . . They're all here for you. . . . When we put the word out, the requests to attend were overwhelming. At first it was all the people who work in your companies, or who have ever worked with you. But that was just the start. Then spouses and kids of people who worked with you started calling. They wanted to come too. Then it was all your partners, suppliers, customers . . . All the people whose lives you've made better. They all wanted to be here. They all wanted to thank you."

I looked down at Thomas. For the first time in all the years I'd known him, he was overwhelmed. Tears rolled down his cheeks as he recognized friends and clients and employees who had all gathered to tell him, "You made a difference."

Josephine touched my shoulder. "Keep going," she said gently, and indicated the red carpet. As I rolled Thomas forward, the crowd parted to let us through. I saw Maggie and Kerry standing in front of us on the opposite side of the room. They had an arm around each other and, like almost everyone else in the room, were smiling, laughing, and crying all at the same time as they watched us come forward.

When I rolled Thomas up to them, Kerry hugged him. "We've missed you my friend," she said. Thomas nodded to her. He wanted to respond, but he couldn't.

Maggie leaned down and kissed him. "I love you," she said. "And we've got a little surprise for you." She handed him a gold braid rope that was attached to the top of the corner of the curtain. "This is from all of us to you."

All around us, people were yelling. I could pick out individual voices: "We're here for you, Thomas." "We love you, Thomas."

"Thank you, Thomas."

Kerry put her hand on Thomas's shoulder. "Open the curtain." She smiled, nodding in the direction of the crowd of people. "You're driving them crazy."

Thomas pulled down on the gold braid cord, and the curtain swung to the side. Behind it was a beautiful two-story entryway of marble and glass. Above the doors it said *Live every day as if it will become part of the museum of your life.*

The crowd erupted. I had thought it impossible for the noise to get any louder, but I was wrong. Maggie leaned down to Thomas. "Are you ready?"

Thomas's voice was choked with emotion. "I want them to come in with me," he said, and indicated toward the crowd.

"All of them?" I asked.

"All of them."

Kerry opened the double doors and I wheeled Thomas into the opening room. Kerry instructed the group of people closest to the doors to wait just a few minutes and then let everyone in.

In front of us was a giant marble wall with a carved portrait of Thomas and a large block of writing. The text described the approach to life Thomas had taught me on that icy cold morning over a decade earlier:

Imagine if every day of our life was cataloged. The way we felt, the people we saw, how we spent our time. And at the end of our life a museum was built. It was built to show exactly how we lived our life. If eighty percent of our time was at a job we didn't like, then eighty percent of the museum would be dedicated to showing us unhappily spending our time at a job we didn't like.

If we were friendly with ninety percent of the people we interacted with, it would show that. But if we were angry and upset or yelled at ninety percent of the people we interacted with, it would show that. If we loved the outdoors, or spending time with our kids, or celebrating life with our significant other, but only spent two percent of our life fueling those loves, then no matter how much we wished it to be different, only two percent of our museum would be dedicated to that.

Imagine what it would be like to walk that museum toward the end of our life. How would we feel? How would we feel knowing that for the rest of eternity that museum would be how we were remembered? Every person who walked it would know us exactly as we truly were. Our legacy would be based not on how we dreamed of living, but how we lived.

Imagine if heaven, or the afterlife, or however we individually think of it, actually consists of us being the tour guide for our own museum—for all of eternity.

On the next panel of the wall, it said:

This museum is dedicated to Thomas Derale. A man who inspired museum dreams in all of us. A man who encouraged us to live life as it should be lived, so that at the end, each of our lives would be a success as we individually defined success. He has been many things to all of us. Not the least of which, he has been the greatest leader in the world. We dedicate this museum to him. It is the museum of his life.

Below the text were signatures. Thousands upon thousands of them.

A tear rolled from the corner of my eye and down my cheek. I looked at the others. Everyone was crying.

"Please let the others in," Thomas said, his voice choked with emotion. "I want them to see how much this means to me."

For the next two hours, we walked Thomas through the museum of his life. Each stop brought forth memories and stories. People were waiting at specific pictures and exhibits so they could tell Thomas what those moments with him had meant in their lives. As I watched Thomas that afternoon, I saw a soul glowing with the recognition of all his life had been—the people he had touched, the moments he had created. It was watching someone in his finest light. It was perfection.

True to his original idea, the content of the museum was dedicated to how Thomas lived his life. Maggie had worked with Kerry, and an entire section was filled with pictures and notes chronicling the places Maggie and Thomas had traveled together, and the experiences they'd had.

Individual rooms were created for each of Thomas's core philosophies. In the room titled "Fulfilling Your Big Five for Life," entire exhibits showed how people had been impacted by Thomas's ideas. They included family pictures, college diplomas, postcards from exotic places people had traveled to, and an entire wall of funny photos people had taken of each other performing their roles in Thomas's companies.

As we rounded a large-curved corner, in front of us was an entire curving wall full of baby pictures. "This idea came from so many people it just had to be here," Maggie said to Thomas. "Your fellow travelers wanted you to know that your philosophies, the culture you created, the flexibility you allowed people, and the opportunities you gave them were a big part of what inspired them to bring these little ones into the world."

Next to the pictures, people had posted brief narratives about the way Thomas had impacted their experiences as a parent. Some talked about how they were able to spend time with their babies when they were born. Others talked about being able to attend Little League games. Many of them thanked Thomas for inspiring them with things they then taught their children.

One room was wall-to-wall original Post-it notes Thomas had left for people over the years and they had saved. There were thank-you ones, jokes, notes of encouragement.

Another section of the museum was dedicated to Thomas's five-pillar model. The many companies he had partnered with over the years had put together a hilarious sculpture showing Thomas resting in a reclining sun chair on top of a circular platform supported by five Gothic pillars. Sculpted shark fins were weaving in and out of the waves at the base of the pillars. Next to Thomas was a giant bottle of shark repellent, and the ingredients label listed each of his four steps to boosting profits along with a description of each one.

The inscription near the exhibit read:

To a man who has encouraged and enabled us to fulfill our own Purposes For Existing. You have been a pillar, a partner, and always a friend. We could have covered these walls with clippings of the deals we've made together or the contracts we've signed; the charts showing how our stocks grew because of the ideas you shared with us at Fulfill U; or our annual reports showing our increased revenues because we always knew we could count on you to deliver for us, which enabled us to deliver for our customers.

We felt, though, this more accurately represents what your true impact on all of us has been. At different times in our lives, and in different ways, you helped each of us remember that work did not have to be a means to an end. That if we chose the right work, it was, in large part, the end itself.

It was signed by the owners and employees from hundreds of organizations Thomas's companies had partnered with during his life.

The walls surrounding the pillar sculpture were covered in e-mails, faxes, and letters customers had sent in thanking the different companies for what they'd done. There were pictures of people laughing and having fun in their offices and at their company events, and awards the organizations had won for ingenuity, customer service, and dedication. One creatively designed section was a collage of smiling individuals, from many different organizations, who were all being recognized for their years of service.

Chapter Thirty-five

LATER THAT EVENING, AFTER EVERYONE HAD walked through the museum and then celebrated at the event that followed, Thomas asked me to wheel him back down to the museum. It was empty now and mostly dark. The only illumination was from the individual accent lights for each of the displays. Thomas took time in front of each exhibit, reading the messages, feeling the emotions behind them. I rolled him from one to the next. Neither of us spoke much. It was quiet now, and I got the impression that as he passed each section, Thomas was saying good-bye.

In the rush of the crowd during the afternoon, I hadn't had a chance to read the inscription on the plaque just before the exit door. We were paused before it now. The small sign next to the plaque was simple—Thomas Derale's final memo to his fellow travelers. It was dated six weeks earlier and titled "This is what you've taught me."

Thomas spoke quietly, "When I found out I was dying, I wrote this and asked Kerry to give it to each of our people. I wanted to leave them with something. I hope it was enough."

I looked at the plaque and began to carefully read each word.

A successful leader starts with something so linked to their own Purpose For Existing that what they pursue is not just an opportunity, it is a personal necessity. They have enough confidence in their own abilities that they feel validated, not threatened, by the successes of those they are leading. They encourage, not belittle; inspire, not intimidate; teach, not obstruct; anticipate success, not fear failure.

At every moment during our existence we are all called to be leaders, if for no other purpose than to lead ourselves.

When I finished reading, I put my hand on Thomas's shoulder. "It's perfect Thomas. . . . It's perfect."

Thomas reached into the pocket of his shirt and pulled out a pack of his personalized Post-it notes. "Old habit." He smiled and took out a pen and started to write. When he finished, he stared up at the plaque for a few moments, then took a long look back at the rest of the museum.

"It's time to go, Joe."

As I started to wheel him toward the door, he pulled off the Post-it note, and as we passed next to the plaque, he put the note underneath it.

I love you all.
—Thomas

Epilogue

FIVE DAYS AFTER WE WHEELED HIM INTO THE museum of his life, Thomas Derale passed away. I lost a friend, a mentor, and we all lost the greatest leader in the world.

In the days that followed, I found myself in a deep depression. I knew I shouldn't be. I knew Thomas wouldn't have wanted it that way. But I missed him. I just missed him.

Almost two months after his death, I received a box in the mail. Inside was a note from Maggie and a small package.

Dear Joe,

Toward the very end, Thomas made me promise I would get this to you. He worked on it tirelessly when he was first diagnosed, and even while you were here. I don't know why, but for some reason he wanted to share this with you in this way. I helped him finish it in the days just before his death. You were a great friend to him, Joe, and he valued that friendship tremendously.

With love,
Maggie

Taped to Maggie's note was an envelope. I removed the card inside.

Dear Joe,

During our many discussions, you often asked me about my story. How did I become the person I am? What shaped my life? Where did it all begin? I'm afraid despite all those discussions, the full details of that story are something I never had the chance to share with you. There was always so much else to talk about, to laugh about, to dream into reality . . .

I apologize for that, and I hope this will suffice. Be well, Joe, and thanks. Next to my love of Maggie, your friendship is one of the things that has meant the most to me during my journey.

Your friend and fellow traveler,

Thomas

I unwrapped the package that had been inside the box, and immediately a smile formed on my lips. It was a book, and the author was Thomas Derale.

I sat back in my chair, opened to the first page, and began to read.

Thank you for reading

THE

BIG FIVE

for LIFE

There are many options for you to continue this adventure.

Join us for the annual Big Five for Life™ Leadership Summit and meet other Big Five for Life™ type of leaders.

Get a jump start on your own Big Five for Life™ at one of our Big Five for Life™ Discovery courses.

Invite author John P. Strelecky to speak at your organization.

Receive a free copy of John's articles on- Succeeding in Life and Business

For more information about all of these, please visit:

www.bigfiveforlife.com

Thomas Derale Takeaways

1. A successful leader starts with something so linked to their own Purpose For Existing that what they pursue is not just an opportunity, it is a personal necessity. They have enough confidence in their own abilities that they feel validated, not threatened, by the successes of those they are leading. They encourage, not belittle; inspire, not intimidate; teach, not obstruct; anticipate success, not fear failure. At every moment during our existence we are all called to be leaders, if for no other purpose than to lead ourselves.

2. Nothing halts progress like someone who is either in the wrong spot or discontent simply for the sake of being discontent. It's demoralizing to others, and it draws energy and time from the tasks being attempted. You want good counterpoint people on your team. People who say, "I know what we're all trying to do, and I think there is a better way." That's valuable in helping make sure the team is on the right track. However, people who just regularly say, "We'll never get there," or who

have no genuine interest in what they do each day, or what the team is trying to do—they simply hold everyone back. And they're also holding themselves back. You have to move them off the team or they'll destroy the team.

3. Fear leads to failure, and fearless leads to success.

4. People can find solutions to almost any problem, but they need to know the rules of the game. Too often people are given a task, and then weeks into the project they present their work to a senior person, only to be informed they need to change direction because of something they were never told about. That's demoralizing and it's costly in terms of people's time, effort, and productivity.

5. Not all customers are looking for the same thing. Instead of offering one type of product or service and losing customers to your competitors, be your own competitor. Cannibalize your own business to yourself.

6. Talented people don't need someone monitoring their behavior. They don't do a great job because someone's watching them. They do a great job because that's who they are, and they like what they do.

7. Everything in my companies is tied to people's Purpose For Existing and Big Five for Life. We do things because in doing them we are guaranteeing our life is a success as we define success. I don't want people working with me who *like* their job. I want people whose work *fulfills* them. When you have that, people don't get burned out each day. They get energized.

8. The incorrect belief I see a lot of is that profits and satisfied people are inversely proportional. Too many leaders think the harder you drive people, the more they will do, and therefore the higher the profits will be. They also think the more satisfied people are, the less someone must be driving them, and therefore profits will be less. The truth is, if you have to drive people that hard to do their job, then you've either got the wrong people, or you've got the right people doing the wrong job.

9. When companies that (a) hired not on job fit, but on how a person would fit with the company's culture, (b) didn't micromanage, but instead gave people greater autonomy and let them manage themselves, and (c) motivated not through money, but by creating a "familylike" environment, were compared to companies that did the opposite of those three, they had 22 percent higher sales growth, 23 percent higher profit growth, and 67 percent lower employee attrition.

10. Two big factors impact profits as they relate to people. The first is productivity—how effective people are. The second is attrition—how often people quit and therefore need to be replaced.

11. If everyone is working as a collective team on a common journey, and one of the common goals of the team is to maximize the organization's profits, then in truth everyone is responsible for profits.

12. If you want to be a CEO, you have to be able to figure out if $C + E < O$. C is cost, E is effort, and O is output. Most people

get hung up on the C and E and never look at the O. Those people suffer from Leftsideitis—they only focus on the left side of the equation.

13. Without profits a company can't function. If a company can't function, no one can get paid. And if no one can get paid, no matter how fulfilled they are, the people won't be able to stick around long. Pretty soon you have no people, no products, no customers, and no company. Everyone's a loser. But if the company is always profitable, then the people can get paid for doing things that fulfill them, the customers are happy, and everyone's a winner.

14. If people can be successful doing things they don't really care about, then they should be wildly successful at something that actually matters to them. And if they are wildly successful, the company will be too, which means big profits and big successes all the way around.

Thomas Derale Takeaways (Continued)

Productivity Assessment Tool for Leaders

Fill in your answer for each question. One is the low end of the scale, and ten is the high end. For example, with the first question of— People are enthused when they show up on a Monday morning—a 1 would indicate not enthused at all, and a 10 would indicate they are extremely enthused. When you have filled in all the questions, take the total number at the bottom and multiply by 2. That gives you an easy way to figure out productivity on a scale of 1–100.

Productivity Question	Ranking 1–10 (1 is low productivity, 10 is high)
1. People are enthused when they show up on a Monday morning.	
2. People perform their tasks without someone watching over them. They don't try to get out of doing what they are supposed to be doing. (For example, excessive social discussions, lunch breaks, wandering the halls…)	
3. People understand the PFE of the organization (could be department, division, etc., depending on the level of leader doing the assessment).	
4. People understand how what they do helps the organization fulfill its PFE.	
5. People are fulfilling their own PFE through the job they get paid to do. (If you don't think people understand their own PFE, this gets a 1.)	
Total	

Thomas Derale Takeaways (Continued)

Ascending Life Curve

This is how most people go through life. Over time they have highs, and they have lows. But in general, their highs are about the same high, and their lows are about the same low. They just oscillate between these two points.

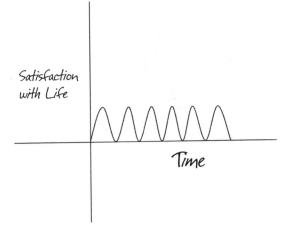

The secret to life is to have a sine curve that doesn't just go on over time, but that ascends over time. It's called an ascending life curve and looks like the one below. In these people's lives, as time goes by, they don't just oscillate between a set of highs and lows, but they keep reaching new highs. Everybody has lows. It happens. Even when you're on the right journey, and heading in the direction you want to go, there are still lows.

But the point is, when you're on an ascending life curve, at some moment in time, your lows are now higher than what used to be your highs. And the way to do that is actually simple. The more moments of your day you spend on something that fulfills your Purpose For Existing, and the more moments each day you spend on your Big Five for Life, the more your life curve ascends.

Being a successful leader is simply a matter of understanding this concept, then applying it.

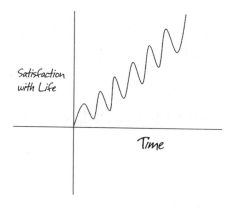

Interested in sharing
The Big Five for Life with others?

To learn about our discounts on bulk purchases of ten or more copies, please e-mail us at:

orders@aspenlightpublishing.com

Ready for your next
adventure?

LIFE
SAFARI

John P. Strelecky

Aspen Light Publishing

From the author of the international bestsellers *The Why Café* and *The Big Five for Life* comes an inspiring and emotionally powerful story set amidst the mystery, beauty, and allure of Africa.

Jack is a young man struggling to find happiness in his life. Although he doesn't know why, the one image that seems to capture his soul is that of Africa. With solitary focus, he saves for two years and then embarks on a journey to find the source of the calling he has felt.

Halfway around the world, a very old, very wise African woman named Ma Ma Gombe is on a journey of her own. She is seeking a fabled destination she was told of as a child—"a place where you can see the earth be born, and then watch the world go to sleep, a place so beautiful that words cannot describe it." It is a destination known to her only as "the birthplace of all."

As if their paths were destined to intertwine, these two unlikely travelers meet shortly after Jack's arrival in Africa and join together on a journey that changes both of their lives forever.

Walk with them as they cross the African continent on foot. Marvel with them at the animals they encounter, the people they meet, and the adventures they experience. Like Jack, find through the teachings of Ma Ma Gombe that piece of your soul yearning to be set free.

In *Life Safari*, John P. Strelecky has created a story that inspires and taps the spirit for adventure in readers everywhere. A tale that will touch your emotions, open your eyes to the amazing continent of Africa, and open your heart to the amazing potential within all of us.

1

I picked up the leather-bound notebook that had been my constant companion throughout the journey. The pages were weather-beaten and torn from the effects of rain and sun and the sheer challenges that came with crossing a continent on foot.

Much had transpired since then, but each time I held that journal I was instantly transported back. And each time, the memory began the same way, with my entrance into Africa.

How long ago that seemed, and yet how powerful was the experience—powerful enough that it has remained a permanent part of my soul. After all, I almost died there. After all, I found my life there.

I didn't know what to expect when I began my journey to Africa. Other than pictures I had seen in books, I knew almost nothing about the people, the animals, or the environment I would encounter. But at the time, none of that seemed to matter. I knew one thing, and that one thing was enough. I knew I needed to be happy. For some reason, I thought Africa was the place where I would find my happiness.

I opened the journal. There it was: Day 1. I had noted it as such with a single statement. "Today, the adventure begins." And indeed it had. I crossed to Africa by ship. The journey took the better part of three weeks. When I left home, I carried nothing more than a large backpack full of clothes, basic camping supplies, good hiking boots, an oversized hat to protect myself from the sun, and the money I'd saved over the course of two years.

Two years was the time it took me to go from the start of my dream to the beginning of my reality. Two years may seem like a long time to wait to pursue one's dream, but not when compared to the lifetime most people spend. Many a person during those two years had expressed how they also would love to go to Africa. Initially I tried to explain that if I could do it so could they. I certainly wasn't the highest paid person among them. As a matter of fact, I was probably one of the lowest.

But I soon realized that they weren't truly serious about going to Africa, or else they would be going. They liked to talk about their dreams, but in the end, they just left them as dreams. They didn't know what I had felt a glimpse of, and what Ma Ma Gombe would confirm for me. That dreams are in fact realities waiting to happen. But they don't wait forever. At some point you have to help them make the transition. Or eventually, they just fade away.

So there I stood, a six-foot-one-inch, twenty-two-year-old kid. Having been an athlete most of my life, I was relatively lean but muscular. To a stranger I would have seemed quietly confident without

being cocky—a little unsure of my future and yet hopeful that I was heading in the right direction.

My ancestors had come from Eastern Europe, and I'd inherited the genes of a mix of nations. My blonde hair and blue eyes were like my mother's, my ability to tan quickly to a deep brown hue reflected more of my father's family.

And there I was—in Africa.

To continue this Africa adventure, visit

www.thelifesafari.com

About the Author

JOHN P. STRELECKY IS THE #1 BESTSELLING author of four books, including *The Big Five for Life*.

In addition to being translated into twenty-one languages and sold in over forty countries, John's works have been distributed to employees of numerous companies, including IBM, American Express, Boeing, Estee Lauder, and many more. They have also been made required course reading at universities around the country.

John holds an MBA from one of the top programs in the world—Northwestern University's Kellogg School of Management—and has served as a strategic advisor to leaders around the globe.

He has been honored alongside Oprah Winfrey, Tony Robbins, Stephen R. Covey, and Wayne Dyer, as one of the one hundred most influential thought leaders in the field of leadership and personal development.

When he isn't writing or speaking, John spends extensive time traveling. He and his wife's longest trip was an almost year long backpacking adventure covering more than seventy thousand miles (almost three times the circumference of the earth). He has taken additional extended trips to the Amazon Basin, Yucatán Peninsula, Central America and China.

In 2009, John began offering immersion experiences for people interested in discovering and fulfilling their Big Five for Life. These Discovery Courses are now offered in the United States and other countries around the world.

He also hosts an annual Big Five for Life Leadership Summit. At this event, leaders operating in the spirit of the Big Five for Life, gather to learn from each other and share their experiences.

Additional details about John and the programs he offers can be found at:

www.bigfiveforlife.com